This book is dedicated to
Emilia and Bruno,
... exemplary parents, and to
Ricky and Paola, ... lights of my life.

A Joan & Jack
new "Amici del Premonte"
focis of Italy

Gianni Carlo

The idea for this book,
a book about undiscovered Piedmont,
about the traditions and culinary delights of this
region, came from you and people who,
like you, are visitors to the area.
So often it is the tourist who brings a sense of
marvel and gusto to the appreciation of a place.

Piedmont is, of course, a very special place,
a treasure-chest for the discerning tourist
despite the fact that there are few
published manuals which truly encompass
all that is has to offer: from food and drink
to food for thought.
The aim of this book is to give the reader a taste of
Piedmont, in every sense and for every sense.
We have tried to transmit the enthusiasm
we ourselves felt at the end of a gastronomic day out!
As the visitor gets to know the wine producers,
restaurant owners and other tourist
operators in the area,
he or she will get an idea of what it means
to feel part of the Piedmontese family,
to feel truly at home.

This is our aim: to enable the reader
to share with us the riches Piedmont
has to offer
and to become a connoisseur
of all things Piedmontese!

The Editor   The Author
Giacomo Soncini   Carlo Zarri

CARLO ZARRI

PIEDMONT

*A journey through
the region's garden
of delights*

Preface

Piero Gros

Welcome to Piedmont

OMEGA EDIZIONI

We felt very strongly that this book should be prefaced by someone with an impeccable Piedmontese pedigree.

PIERO GROS, winner of Olympic gold at Innsbruck in 1976 in the special slalom, is just that.

He is also universally known and appreciated in the sporting world for his sportsmanship and humanity.

Piero's other titles include: winner of the World Skiing Cup in 1974, 12 other firsts at World Champion level, Silver in the slalom at the World Championships at Garmisch in 1978 and Bronze at St Moritz in 1974.

Piero was born at Sauze d'Oulx in 1954 and was mayor of his home town for over 5 years.

He now works as commentator for Swiss television, following all major skiing events at world level.

He is also responsible for organising volunteers in the committee for the 20th Winter Olympics, to be held in Turin in 2006. His home town will be hosting the free-style events during the Olympics.

In his spare time, Piero is involved in the raising of funds for cancer research.

Orsiera-Roccavrè National Park (Susa Valley)
The roe deer's mountain path.

*As someone who has
always been profoundly fascinated
with the beauty of my region,
its wines and other gastronomic delights,
I am more than enthusiastic to present
Carlo's book and to*

welcome you all to Piedmont!

*When I still skied at world class level, people often used to ask
me how I managed to resist the temptation of all those goodies
my mother and grandmother would prepare for me whenever I
went back home to the Susa valley.*

*My reply was that I didn't need to resist a thing because our
cuisine was just perfect for an uthlete's requirements: simple, of
excellent quality and using all fresh ingredients.*

That's what we're used to in Piedmont!

*If anything, difficulties arose when we went racing abroad.
And our foreign colleagues were always enthusiastic at the prospect of competing in Italy and the possibility of a plate of spa-
ghetti dressed with fresh tomato sauce, parmesan and a good
olive oil or some other tasty dish - not to mention, at the end of
the meal, a nice creamy cappuccino.*

*What do a Grand Chef and a world class athlete have in
common?*

*Well, they both need talent, passion, creativity and prepara-
tion, in my opinion. This is the key to success.*

*These days my job allows me to travel the world and I've
observed that sport, tourism and cuisine make the perfect trio
when it comes to a holiday or even just a brief sojourn.*

*It is for these 3 very good reasons that I'd like to invite you
all to come to Piedmont!*

Piero Gros

*W*hat does Piedmont offer the visitor?
Art, culture, lakes, mountains and unspoilt countryside, this is truly Piedmont.
But Piedmont is also full of charming villages, each with its traditions and typical dishes, an irresistible combination for any visitor.

From its capital city, Turin, to Bergolo, the tiniest of villages high in the Alta Langa area; from the village of San Giulio on the banks of Lake Orta to the famous spa town of Acqui, Piedmont offers a cornucopia for the senses. Let's take a look at a few examples:

For our sense of **sight** there are the beautiful views over the snow-tipped Alps, the green of vineyard-covered valleys in the region's south or the blue of its many lakes.

For our sense of **touch** there is the gold finery produced by the master jewellers of Valenza or the high-quality fabrics of Piedmont's textile industries.

For our sense of **smell**, there is the sublime perfume of the truffles from the Alba area, which pervade the town's streets and piazzas and the surrounding countryside during the season.

For our sense of **hearing**, there are the many sounds which typify the region: the pealing of church bells, the tinkling of sheep-bells and the rhythmical labour of the contadino.

For our sense of **taste** there are the many and varied delights of local cuisine.

For those who, like me, do not possess Piedmontese roots, but who have had the good fortune to live in the area, one's conscience is divided: on the one hand, there is the temptation to keep everything for oneself, on the other, the desire to share these immense riches with the rest of the world, convinced of their enormous value. After all, what can possibly give more pleasure than the act of sharing moments of joy with friends and dear ones?

Bergolo in the Alta Langa area: a stone-built village full of light, sound and colour.

My first encounter with Piedmont was at Cortemilia in the province of Cuneo, where my father's family had lived for at least 6 generations. My first impression was truly unforgettable and I knew that my life would never be the same again.

We were waiting at the level crossing at Bistagno, the guleway to the Bormida valley, steeply-sided and dominated by ancient stone watch-towers. Fascinated, I observed the virtually uninhabited castles and villages, the valley slopes chequered with green pasture, alternating with woods, hazel groves and stone terracing - a memory of far-gone days- still bearing traces of vineyards. Here, peace could still be found. This is the thought that springs to mind when contemplating the Langa for the very first time.

> The inhabitants are a straightforward
> and welcoming people with strong ties
> to their traditions and proud of their roots.
> They are the ones who,
> in a completely spontaneous fashion,
> have preserved this
> atmosphere of peace and time
> standing still - both in short supply
> in the world of today.

In fact, during my first contact with the area, I felt like a child again, in touch with nature, the sounds of which pervaded everything: cockcrow in the morning or the hooting of the owl at night. Then there was the freedom to leave the front door of the house unlocked, or to ride a bike without ever having to worry about the traffic. All new experiences for me, a city-dweller.

And then, of course, there was my Aunt Maria's cake to dip in my breakfast mug of milk, which always tasted so particularly delicious!

Not to mention the delights of crusty bread or the ravioli 'al plin' whose only fault was that they came to an end too soon, or the tasty snacks of local 'tuma' cheese and bread and salami which we ate while picking hazels in mid-summer.

Estella Canziani
(early 20ᵗʰ century Pragelato Susa Valley)
Daily Bread

All these memories came flooding back with Fellini-esque intensity.

Now, 20 years on, rural Piedmont has changed very little.

In fact, since the end of the push to modernise at any cost, typical of the '70s, there has been a move to rediscover ancient traditions.

For example, in the place of reinforced concrete, younger generations have preferred to build their houses in the traditional Langa stone.

There has also been a return to work in the countryside, motivated by the growth of a market for quality products. My job allows me to come into contact with people all over the world and I think I can safely assert that all those I've met, whether they be Swiss, American, Japanese or British, have confirmed the view that Piedmont is a fascinating place.

A visit to a winery is a commonplace event but here in Piedmont, you might easily be lucky enough to tour the winery of a producer, who, although world-famous, invites you in like an old friend and sits you down to try his wines and have a chat. Wineries are small-scale here and often the producer lives above his cellars. And who cares if you don't want to buy because you can't take bottles onto the plane? The important thing is to get to know one another!

Another Piedmontese experience, is to phone a restaurant with a magazine-cover chef to book a table and find that you are speaking to the King of Cuisine in person - it really does happen that way in Piedmont!

A candle used for examining wine's visual characteristics lights up the oak barrels used for ageing the wine.

You can get to know Piedmont by dropping in on a country-folk's family, a pastry-cook or a wine producer. This is how: between a mouthful of Barbera and a nibble of a 'Brut e Bon' hazelnut biscuit or a slice of traditional salami, you'll soon discover the family's history, or a story about a larger-than-life figure from the past or a legend of the hills. This is truly Piedmont!

Piedmont is love of life, love of travel, love of art. It has something for all, with its mountains, lakes and traditional cuisine.

Its towns and cities of artistic interest, as is true for the rest of Italy, are blessed with a centuries-long patrimony, especially florid during the long reign of the royal Savoy family.

It was under their reign that Italy was unified and Turin became the country's first capital city, thereby benefiting from the construction of numerous palaces, churches, parks and other monuments of rare beauty and elegance.

Turin's splendid artistic heritage is now being restored to its former glory as this post-industrial city rediscovers its past.

The Baroque style is particularly evident, with its harmonious, elegant lines a unifying feature.

The city's famous architects, Garove, Vitozzi, Castellamonte, Guarini, Benedetto Alfieri and Filippo Juvarra, have all contributed to Turin's development from ancient medieval city, built over the ruins of a Roman encampment, to the city we see today, a vibrant and fascinating place.

All Piedmont is famous for its wines and cuisine, which are particularly to be appreciated towards the south, in the provinces of Alessandria, Asti and Cuneo.

A view of Piazza Castello (Castle Square) in Turin: at
the far end the palace of King Vittorio Emanuele III can be seen;
on the left is the chapel of the Holy Shroud
and the cupola of the church of San Lorenzo.
On the right the facade of Madama Palace is visible.

Turin cathedral which houses the Holy Shroud.

This area, mostly hilly, vaunts products of the very highest quality.

The purity of the air and the richness of the soil guarantee fruit and vegetables of incomparable flavour.

Such is the specificity of the area's characteristics that the same stock, planted elsewhere, does not produce the same qualities.

In the same way, the cheese and other products made from milk produced from animals raised on the high pastures of the area's hills and mountains, contains flavours available nowhere else. Piedmont's famous breeds of cows and sheep give meat which is not only of the highest quality, but is also subjected to the most scrupulous testing in matters of hygiene at farm level and which is rightfully appreciated by gourmets all over the world.

The same can be said for the region's poultry.

It should also be mentioned that Piedmont is among Italy's foremost regions in the use of biological and natural methods of animal farming.

From the tourist's point of view though, food alone is not sufficient to draw one to the area.

There has to also be the prospect of unspoilt countryside, composed of an uninterrupted succession of hills and valleys of breathtaking beauty scattered with artistic and historical sites of the first order.

Not to mention the traditional festivals in costume.

The Piedmontese Alps, rich in national parks and splendid peaks, cover approximately one third of the region's total area. They stretch from the Maritime Alps along the border with the region of Liguria to the Formazza valley which penetrates deep into the heart of Switzerland.

The transparent mist of our valleys.

The mountain peaks, which rise to over 4000 m, are pristine white in the winter and a blue-green during the summer. These mountains are a paradise for any skier from December through to April. From May to September they can be enjoyed by hikers and anyone who loves living in close contact with nature.

Excellent ski resorts can be found, within the Mondovì area in the province of Cuneo, at the so-called '7 sisters' of Pratonevoso, Lurisia, Artesina Frabosa, San Giacomo di Roburent, Garessio, Pamparato and Chiusa Pesio. There is fine skiing to be had through Mon Viso and the Olympic Alps of Sestriere, right over to Monte Rosa in Biella province.

The refuges and mountain stations are connected by trails and paths of varying difficulty and are ideal for whoever wants to admire the abundant wildlife in its natural habitat.

Piedmont's **lakes**: Maggiore, Orta, Mergozzo, Viverone and many others, have been described in the past as "blue diamonds set in the emerald green of nature" and have much to offer in the way of art, history and botanical gardens.

In addition to typical lakeside holidays, our lakeland offers all the delights of Piedmontese culture and tradition: each ancient village has its very own seasonal speciality to charm the discerning tourist.

Estella Canziani
Carnival costumes and masks

THE CITIES, TOWNS, VILLAGES AND COUNTRYSIDE OF PIEDMONT:

TURIN
ALESSANDRIA
ASTI
BIELLA
CUNEO
NOVARA
VERCELLI

A view of Turin's symbolic building, the Mole Antonelliana, as seen from the Monte dei Cappuccini (Mount of the Capuchins) with a backdrop of the Cozie Alpine range.

TURIN

*F*ounded in 28 B.C by the Roman Emperor
Caesar Octavius Augustus, Turin's original name
was Augusta Taurinorum. The city was built
for reasons of military strategy in the shelter
of a hill on the banks of the Po, a navigable river.

In 1561, Turin became the capital of the Sabauda Dukedom
under Emanuele Filiberto of Savoy. From this moment, Turin's
importance grew in a economic, political and historical sense.
Its modern-day appearance is due predominantly to 3 separate
periods of expansion during the Baroque era of the Sabauda
Court.

The first was planned by Carlo Emanuele I of Savoy and executed between 1619 and 1622 by the architect Carlo di
Castellamonte who built San Carlo square and Via Roma. Via
Roma's present-day appearance is due to reconstruction during
the Fascist era of 1931 - 37.

The second period of expansion developed the city towards the
east. This occurred during the reign of Carlo Emanuele II and
was executed by the architect Amedea di Castellamonte. In
1673 he built Carlo Emanuele square, now known as Piazza
Carlina and Via Po, the street which connected the royal residences in Piazza Castello to the river.

The last period of expansion was in 1716 during the reign of
King Vittorio Amedeo II. The architect Filippo Juvarra developed the so-called Military Quarters and, following the style of
the French Court, also developed the King's numerous subur-
ban residences and embellished the Royal Palace and other buildings belonging to the Royalty.

During the 19th century, with the arrival of Napoleon followed by the Restoration of the Monarchy, the Wars of
Independence and, finally, in 1861 the Unification of Italy,
Turin underwent an artistic decline. Later, it became an important industrial centre with the foundation, in 1899, of the Fiat
car factory followed, 10 years later, with that of the Lancia car
factory.

Now, at the beginning of the 21st century, Turin is redisco-
vering its cultural and artistic heritage. Thanks to both public

and private funding, countless Baroque palaces have been restored to their former glory. The Sabauda palaces are now open to
the public and there are dozens of museums and art galleries to
visit. For the tourist, Turin is a happy combination of art, culture and entertainment.

Antonello da Messina
Portrait of a Man, 1476 - Oil on wood 36.5 x 27.5 x 6 cm
Donated by the city of Milan in 1935.
The artistic symbol of Turin, this masterpiece was
a gift from Milan's Trivulzio Collection with the collaboration of P. Accorsi.
It is exhibited in the Museum of Ancient Art housed in Madama Palace.

THE SABAUDA RESIDENCES

*ℳost of these splendid gems of Baroque
architecture, complete with antique furnishings
and important works of art, are now open to the public.*

'*Palazzo Reale*', the Royal Palace, in 'Piazza Castello' (the
castle square), was built by Emanuele Filiberto of Savoy. The
influence of Filippo Juvarra is to be noted inside the palace, with
the famous 'scala delle forbici' or 'scissors stairway' not to mention the 'chinoiserie' popular in this period, particularly evident
in the splendid 'Chinese Room'. The influence of other important artists may also be seen, such as the cabinet maker Pietro
Piffetti, maestro of Rococo inlaying, the Piedmontese pictorial
artists Beaumont and Cignaroli or the work of Pelagio Pelagi
from Bologna, who designed the wrought-iron gates of the
Palace.

Palazzo Madama, situated next to Palazzo Reale, now
houses the Civic Art Gallery. The site was originally Roman,
corresponding to the eastern 'Porta Decumana'. The 2 towers
are of medieval origin whereas the building's facade, with its
play on space and fullness, aiming at perfect architectural harmony, was redesigned by Juvarra in the 18*th* century.

Palazzo Carignano on Via Accademia delle Scienze, is an
extraordinary example of Baroque architecture by Guarino
Guarini who came to Turin in 1666. Built in stone with the
undulating convex and concave lines of its facade, it now houses the Soprintendenza per i Beni Artistici e Storici del
Piemonte (the regional office for artistic and cultural heritage)
and the museum of the Italian Risorgimento.

On the banks of the river Po is the 17*th* century **Valentino
Castle**, which had its heyday under Queen Maria Cristina of
France who used it for her court receptions. Under her guidan-
ce, the architects Carlo and Amedeo di Castellamonte richly
decorated the rooms with stuccoes and frescoes with Arcadian,
mythological and floral themes to entertain the members of the
court.

Just outside Turin, in **Stupinigi**, there is the 'Palazzina di
Caccia' or hunting palace of the Savoy family, also built by the

great Filippo Juvarra. The design includes a central part with two adjacent wings. Splendidly furnished, the King's and Queen's apartments are decorated with frescoes, as is the lovely elliptical ballroom, which, with its great windows facing onto the park, offered a spectacular backdrop of art and nature for court entertainments.

Other sites of interest are the castle at Racconigi, which contains furnishings dating from the 17th and 18th centuries and is situated in abundant parkland and the **castle at Rivoli**, today home to a collection of modern art, dominating the city from its hill.

Last but not least, is the **Reggia di Venaria**, recently restored to its former glory. Here, we can admire the famous Diana gallery, designed by Castellamonte and restructured by Juvarra, another Baroque gem, which, with its play of light at the building's entrance, represented the splendour of the monarchy.

ARTISTIC AND CULTURAL HERITAGE

*Turin is home to many art galleries and museums. Among the most prominent is the **Egyptian Museum**, second in the world only to the museum in Cairo for the value of its exhibits. Here, over 30 000 artefacts are displayed, including a black granite statue of Rameses II, the architect Kha's tomb and many other mummies, sarcophagi and papyri of historical interest.*

The **Turin Museum Foundation** comprises several bodies, including the '**Museo d'Arte Antica di Palazzo Madama**', (the Madama Palace museum art gallery), at present closed to the public, which contains the famous 'Portrait of a Man' by Antonello da Messina, originally belonging to the Trivulzio collection and the '**Galleria d'Arte Moderna e Contemporanea**', gallery of modern art. The latter houses a prestigious collection of works by international artists from the 18th and 19th centuries and also contains the city's best-stocked library of history of art.

The **Sabauda gallery** contains a vast collection of paintings from the 14th through to the 18th centuries, including Dutch, Venetian and Piedmontese masters such as Jan Van Eyck, Rembrandt, Bassano and Veronese. The 'Pinacoteca dell'Accademia Albertina' (Albertina Academy art gallery), includes not only paintings but also drawings such as the 16th century preparatory cartoons by Gaudenzio Ferrari and his school.

Very much in keeping with Turin's Baroque soul is the '**Museo di Arti Decorative di Pietro Accorsi**' (the Pietro Accorsi gallery of decorative arts), which includes the collection left by its patron, a famous antiquarian. Among the many objet d'art are a fine piece by the famous cabinetmaker Pietro Piffetti, inlaid with ivory and tortoiseshell, porcelain treasures from Europe and China and antique furniture of Piedmontese, Venetian and French origin.

Rivoli's castle houses one of Europe's most outstanding collections of **modern art**, with works by Lucio Fontana, Sol Le Witt, Claes Oldemburg, Michelangelo Pistoletto and many others.

Another important gallery of modern art is Turin's **'Fondazione Sandretto Re Rebaudengo'**, (the Sandretto Re Rebaudengo foundation) which closely follows contemporary trends. Well worth a visit is the **'Pinacoteca Giovanni e Marella Agnelli'**, a small but world-renowned gallery founded by the late Gianni Agnelli and containing works by Canaletto, Picasso, Dalì and Matisse. Last but not least the 'Museo del Cinema' (cinema museum) must be mentioned, housed in the Mole Antonelliana, Turin's famous landmark. Here, through the use of daguerreotypes and optical boxes, the visitor is accompanied on a fascinating trip through cinema history.

FOR MORE INFORMATION:
Turismo Torino, via Bogino 8, 10123 Turin - Telephone: 011 883426

The Giovanni and Marella Agnelli Art Collection is situated on the roof of the vast Lingotto complex.

Turin's Egyptian Museum. A spectacular statue of Ramses II in black granite. The pharaoh wears the blue crown and holds the 'hega', or sceptre, symbol of regal power, in his right hand.

Turin's museum of cinema, together with the Lingotto complex, is fast becoming one of the city's main attractions.

CULTURAL TOURS OF TURIN

You will need a whole day to complete this first tour. Start from Piazza Castello with a visit to the Palazzo Reale and the part of Palazzo Madama which is open to the public. Then on to the church of San Lorenzo, built by Guarino Guarini between 1668 and 1687 and the Cappella della Sacra Sindone (Chapel of the Holy Shroud), also completed by Guarini using Castellamonte's project.

In front of the medieval part of Palazzo Madama is the **Archivio di Stato** (State archives) and the **Regio Theatre**, whereas the portico adjacent to the gates of Palazzo Reale, constructed by Pelagio Pelagi, houses the **Biblioteca** (library) and the **Armeria Reale** (Royal Armoury). Now leave the square and proceed down via Po under its portico until, down via Montebello on your left, the **Mole Antonelliana** comes into view. The Mole, built by Alessandro Antonelli, was commissioned as a synagogue in 1863 and is the highest building constructed with masonry in Europe. It now houses the **Museo del Cinema** (museum of cinema) but still contains a glass elevator from which you can admire a wonderful view over the city.

Carry on down the left side of via Po and you will come to the **Museo di Arti Decorative della Fondazione Pietro Accorsi** (the Pietro Accorsi museum of decorative arts). Beyond this, is the great Vittorio Veneto piazza commissioned by Carlo Felice during the period 1825 to 1830. At the far end of the square is the river Po. Pass over the Vittorio Emanuele bridge and you arrive at the **Chiesa della Gran Madre**, an impressive neo-classical church, built against the backdrop of the Turin hills by Ferdinando Bonsignore from 1818 to 1831.

Walk along the banks of the Po to the right of Piazza Vittorio and you will come to the **Valentino park**, a green area of over 550,000 square metres. Within the park you can visit the Valentino **castle** and the **Borgo Medievale**, the medieval quarter, an 18th century folly which contains examples of medieval Piedmontese art.

A few kilometres further down the road and you will arrive at the **Museo dell'Automobile**, the famous Turin car museum. The Lingotto complex is nearby, the ex-industrial zone of Fiat, transformed by the architect Renzo Piano into a centre which includes shops, hotels and other services plus the **Pinacoteca Agnelli**, founded by the Agnelli family.

The second itinerary also requires a whole day. Start from via Roma, Turin's main street, which includes many designer shops and is protected by a long covered walkway built during

Giovanni Michele Graneri (18ᵗʰ century)
The Market in San Carlo Square, Turin (1752).
Oil on canvas 153 x 205cm.
Acquired by P. Accorsi in 1931 on behalf of the Turin Civic Gallery of Modern Art.

San Carlo Square. This little-known fresco depicts the Holy
Shroud, symbol of popular devotion. It can be seen on the corner
with Via Alfieri. Its counterpart is to be found on the other side of
the square, on the corner with Via Santa Teresa.

the 1930s and you will soon arrive in **Piazza San Carlo**, *masterpiece of Piedmontese baroque architecture designed by Carlo di Castellamonte. Here you can admire the twin churches of* **San Carlo** *and* **Santa Cristina***. Now follow via Maria Vittoria to your left and you will arrive in via Accademia delle Scienze, where the* **Egyptian museum** *and the* **Sabauda art gallery** *are situated. Also open to the public is* **Palazzo Carignano** *which houses the* **museum of the Italian Risorgimento***. Now turn back onto via Maria Vittoria and you can visit the baroque church of* **San Filippo Neri***, which contains some interesting paintings. If you now turn back onto via Accademia delle Scienze, you arrive in Piazza Castello and from here, via Garibaldi. To the right of this street is a fascinating area of narrow and winding lanes known as the 'quadrilatero romano' or Roman quarter which also contains several splendid baroque churches. Following via Milano, you arrive at the* **Porta Palazzo** *open market, largest of its kind in Europe. In the adjacent street, via Borgo Dora, an antiques and bric-a-brac market, known as the* **'Balon'** *is held every Saturday and Sunday. Now turn back into via Garibaldi in the direction of Piazza Statuto. If you enter the streets to your right you can visit* **Palazzo Barolo** *with its 17th and 18th century apartments,* **Palazzo Martini di Cigala** *and* **Piazza Savoia** *with its obelisk. Here you will also find the historical* **Santuario della Consolata***, dear to the people of Turin. There are many interesting wineries and other ethnically diverse shops and restaurants to visit in this area.*

Carignano Palace.

POPULAR FAITH

The religious devotion of the people of Piedmont is amply demonstrated by the construction, throughout the region, of sanctuaries and 'sacri monti', or sacred mounts. The periodic exhibition of the Holy Shroud of Turin is another important manifestation.
Over 600 frescoes and paintings also testify to the region's adhesion to the Church,

(see also: 'The Holy Shroud, Images of Christ and Popular Faith' printed by Omega Edizioni).

The Olympic Valleys are home to the **Museum of the Diocese** which is situated in various different sites with the main museum to be found in the town of Susa. The extraordinary cultural and artistic heritage displayed in these museums is representative of many centuries of Catholic devotion.

In the past, the Olympic Valleys represented a natural link between Italy and the rest of Europe. Popes, emperors, annies and pilgrims **all journeyed through these valleys**. Every town possesses a monument or some other object which testifies to their influence: for example, the Abbey of Sant'Antonio of Ranverso or the Bishopric of Susa, as represented by its Museum of Sacred Art. Novalesa is the site of a Benedictine abbey. At Melezet, a hamlet of Bardonecchia, there is a museum displaying a collection of artefacts in gold, wooden statuary and religious ceremonial garments.

FOR INFORMATION CONTACT:
The Cultural Centre of the Diocese (Centro Culturale Diocesano), Via Mazzini 1 - 10059 - (TO)
Telephone and fax: 0122 622610

'The Madonna of the Bridge', a 12th century wooden statue which can be seen in the Museum of the Diocese of Susa. It is just one of many such Madonnas in the diocese's possession. It still bears traces of its original colours and possesses various interesting details: for example, the adult face and hands of the baby Jesus. The statue has been venerated by the faithful for hundreds of years.

THE PROVINCE OF TURIN

Turin province is both large and full of fascinating things to see among which are impressive mountain valleys such the Val di Susa with its ski resorts of Bardonecchia, Cesana, Clavière and Sauze d'Oulx. Sestrière separates it from the Val Chisone, not so well-known perhaps but equally as inviting with its resort, Pragelato. Other interesting valleys to visit are the Val Pellice and the Valli di Lanzo, not forgetting many historical towns and their monuments.

Worthy of note is the town of Susa, with its Roman archway of Augustus and several ancient churches, including San Giusto. The Museo Diocesano, museum of the diocese, is situated in the chiesa del ponte, the church of the bridge and contains many religious objects of interest and value, including gold and sculptures. The Val di Susa contains many abbeys such as the splendid Gothic-Romanesque Sacra di San Michele high on its mountain, monte Pirchiriano, 969 m above sea-level. San'Antonio di Ranversa is to be found further down the valley, near Avigliano and contains beautiful 15th century frescoes by Giacomo Jaquerio, a major Italian Gothic painter. Equally as splendid is the church of San Giovanni with paintings by the 16th century artist Defendente Ferrari.

Pinerolo boasts a Gothic cathedral in its 'centro storico' plus numerous medieval palaces. Not far from the town and dominating it from its hill is the church of San Maurizio, also Gothic, containing altar pieces by Beaumont and Petrini. To be visited are the 14th century palaces Principi d'Acaja and Senato and also the Museo Nazionale dell'Arma di Cavalleria (national museum of the cavalry), documenting 3 centuries of cavalry history in Italy and around Europe. The Forte di Fenestrelle is situated high in the Val Chisone. Building was begun in 1727 by Vittorio Amedeo II and the fort was originally destined as protection against foreign invasion although it was subsequently used mostly as a prison.

On the opposite side of the valley is Chieri, a town with Roman origins which boasts many medieval palaces, such as Palazzo Tana, in its 'centro storico'. The most important building is, however, the cathedral, a splendid example of Gothic Lombard architecture with its magnificent baptistery containing frescoes by the local 14th century artist Guglielmo Fantini. Other frescoes, altar pieces and sculptures can be seen within the cathedral. San Domenico is another splendid Gothic church which also houses 14th century frescoes and some of the painter Guglielmo Caccia's best works. This painter, also known as Moncalvo, ran his workshop in Chieri for several years. Not far away, in the town of Pecetto, more 14th century frescoes by Guglielmo Fantini and others can be admired in the small but attractive cemetery church.

Towards the plain, the town of Moncalieri, which borders on Turin, is worth a visit with its splendid Castello Sabaudo, which can still be visited in part. The 'centro storico' contains many palaces, the most interesting of which is the Palazzo Duc. A must is the church of Santa Maria della Scala with its works by Moncalvo and a very rare example of a 15th or 16th century sandstone sculpture.

Other places to visit in the province of Turin include the Canavese area. Ivrea is home to the church of San Bernardino with a vast and perfectly-preserved cycle of frescoes by the Piedmontese Renaissance master Martino Spanzotti.

Pinerolo: an elegant and refined little town situated
at the mouth of the Chisone Valley. The town's traditions include
printing and the Cavalry School active in the town from 1849 to
1943. There is an interesting equestrian museum to visit plus the
Museum of Military Cavalry (see preceding page.)

Lia Laterza
The Abbey of San Michele (oil on canvas).

ALESSANDRIA AND ITS PROVINCE

Alessandria was founded in 1168 by the Lombard League and Pope Alexander III, from which it derives its name. It is situated on the right bank of the river Tanaro, where it meets the Bormida river and was originally destined as a military centre defending the area from the army of Federico Barbarossa.

The town's most important monument is the Gothic church of **Santa Maria di Castello**, built in the 15th century on the sites of 2 smaller churches, the remains of which can be seen beneath the floor. The **museum** and the **civic art gallery** contain many works of art, including paintings by Luca Cambiaso and 18th century artists from the area, such as Giovanni Migliara, Angelo Morbelli and Giuseppe Pelizza da Volpedo.

The town's 'centro storico' contains **Palazzo Ghilini**, built between 1730 and 1733 by Benedetto Alfieri. A visit to the **Museo del Cappello** (hat museum) is well worth while, reminding us that Alessandria was once world-famous for the production of **Borsalino** felt hats.

Near Alessandria is **Marengo**, where, on June 1st 1800, a bloody battle was fought between the Napoleonic army and Austrian forces. A museum commemorates this tragic event. Nearby is the **Abbey of Santa Croce a Boscomarengo**, built in 1566 by Pope Pius V, Michele Ghislieri, a native of Bosco. Many famous Tuscan, Umbrian and Roman artists were engaged on the unique project, including Egnazio Danti, Martino Longhi and Giorgio Vasari - this last painted a series of important works for the abbey.

The province comprises a part of the Po plain but also the hilly area of the Monferrato. To the south, it is fringed by the imposing Ligurian Apennines. This is an area rich in tradition and culture. Not to be missed is the **Crea Sanctuary**. The original church dates back to the 12th century, although the idea of the sanctuary, which dates from 1589 and was built along the lines of the Varallo sanctuary, is to be attributed to Father Costantino Massimo. In addition to the main church and its 15th century frescoes including an altar piece by Macrino d'Alba, there are other 23 chapels scattered through the woods, mostly dedicated to the Virgin Mary, plus 5 votive shrines dedi-

Santa Croce in Boscomarengo

*An aerial view of Alessandria's 'citadel',
one of the largest 18th century fortifications in Europe.*

cated to saints, all containing frescoes and statues. The most spectacular chapel is known as the '**Paradiso**' or paradise chapel. This is to be found on the top of the hill and houses hundreds of extraordinary terracotta figures mostly made by the Flemish artists Jean and Nicolas Wespin, known as 'i Tabachetti'. It also contains frescoes dating from the 17th century by Giorgio Alberti, a follower of Moncalvo.

Nearby **Casale** is full of interesting monuments, including the Gothic-Romanesque **cathedral**, where a 13th century silver **crucifix** is to be seen, as well as works by Gaudenzio Ferrari and a local 18th century painter, Pietro Francesco Guala. Also worth a visit is the **synagogue**, one of the most prestigious in Italy, and the **civic museum** which houses material of archeological interest, paintings of the Piedmontese school and, above all, works by the sculptor Leonardo Bistolfi (1859 - 1933).

To the south of Alessandria, in **Sezzadio**, is the abbey of **Santa Giustina** with its 14th century frescoes in the Lombard style and, situated on the road to Aqui Terme, at **Cassine**, the church of **San Francesco** also containing many frescoes. The town of **Aqui Terme** is famous for its spa waters. At **Novi Ligure** is the **Oratorio della Confraternità di Maria Maddalena**, whose main feature is a spectacular series of 17th century statues of the crucifixion. **Serravalle Scrivia** has an important Roman archeological site, **Libarna**.

Casale's cathedral.

ASTI AND ITS PROVINCE

settlement at the time of the Ligurian tribes, Asti became a Roman colony in 89 BC, gaining in stature under the Longobards during the 6th to 7th centuries AD.

It was during the 11th century, however, that Asti began to play an increasingly important political and economic role in Piedmont, exceeding that of Turin itself. Some of the many palaces, towers and churches built during this, Asti's heyday, can still be seen. The famous *'Palio'* horse race, held in September and similar to that of Siena, also dates back to the Middle Ages.

Asti's medieval background is still very much in evidence despite much rebuilding during the 18the century. The **baptistery of San Pietro in Consavia** is an example of Romanesque architecture and the **cathedral**, (built during 1327 - 1354), is Lombard Gothic and contains many works of art, including a polyptych and several altar pieces by the 16th century artist Gandolfino da Roveto. Also to be noted are paintings by Guglielmo Caccia, (1568 - 1625), known as Moncalvo, an artist who worked for many years in the Asti and Monferrato area. There are frescoes by the 17th century painters from Lombardy Federico and Salvatore Bianchi and also by the 18th century artist from Como, Carlo Innocenzo Carloni da Scaria.

The church of **San Secondo** (built during 1255 - 1462), is an elegant Gothic building and contains pieces by Gandolfino da Roveto. Among the buildings worth seeing should be mentioned the 16th century **Palazzo Malabaila** and a number of other buildings either built or renovated by Benedetto Alfieri, Asti's great architect and uncle of Vittorio Alfieri, Asti's major poet and dramatist. Among these are **Palazzo Mazzetti** which now houses the **civic art gallery**, **Palazzo Alfieri**, **Palazzo del Seminario** and **Palazzo Ottolenghi**. Palazzo Alfieri houses the **Museo Alfieriano**, a museum dedicated to the poet and a **study centre** in addition to the **library** and l'Istituto per la **Storia della Resistenza e della Società Contemporaneo** (a study centre for the history of the Resistance and contemporary history).

Around Asti, as far as the eye can see, are the gently rolling hills of the **Monferrato** area, with their vineyards and little hilltop villages. Each of these places is full of history, sometimes stretching back thousands of years, as demonstrated by the numerous Romanesque churches, among the most important in

*The San Pietro di Consavia complex,
known as the 'baptistery' by the people of Asti.
This noble Romanesque building has been completely restored.*

the north of Italy. Well worth a visit are the churches of **San Secondo in Cortazzone**, **San Lorenzo in Montiglio**, **Madonna dei Monti** in **Grazzano Badoglio** and the abbey of **Vezzolano** in **Albugnano** with its 13th and 14th century frescoes. Also of interest is the facade of the church at **Roccaverano**. The **shrine at Colle Don Bosco** dedicated to Saint Giovanni Bosco, although modern, is an important place of worship for many.

The province of Asti is home to over 50 castles, including the castle of **Montiglio**, with its **chapel of San Andrea** containing marvellous 13th century frescoes. Other interesting castles are to be found at **Costigliole**, **Castell'Alfero**, **Cortanze** and **Piea**. The latter contains 18th century frescoes by the Galliari brothers, open to the public.

Many of the province's towns possess fascinating and well-preserved historical centres. This is the case at **Moncalvo**, where the painter Guglielmo Caccia lived for many years and where several of his works can be seen in the church of **San Francesco**. In the town of **Aramengo** there is an important workshop for the restoration of works of art run by **Guido and GianLuigi Nicola**.

The vast art restoration workshop belonging to the Nicola family of Aramengo (Asti).

The Martini Enological Museum situated in Pessione.
Sixteen rooms contain exhibits narrating the story of wine in the area
from around 1000 B.C to the present day.

BIELLA AND ITS PROVINCE

*B*iella *became part of the Sabauda dukedom in 1379 and was subsequently nominated provincial capital by King Carlo Emanuele I although it was later amalgamated with the town of Vercelli and did not regain this status until 1996.*

The town's most notable monument is the **baptistery**, built between the end of the 10th and the beginning of the 11th century. The basic structure is square, with semi-circular apses on each side and a tall octagonal roof. Both its ancient origins and a tendency towards the newer Lombard-Romanesque style are evident. The bell-tower of Santo Stefano also dates back to the 11th century. The 16th century **church of San Sebastiano** contains many works of art and the **church of the convent of San Girolamo** houses a splendid wooden choir stall decorated with landscapes by Defendente Ferrari (1523). Among the palaces worth visiting are the 16th century **Palazzo Gromo di Ternengo** with its 2 internal courtyards and **Palazzo Ferrero**.

Typical of this province are its '**Sacri Monti**', or 'sacred mountains', areas where several or many shrines have been built and where art and popular belief meet against a backdrop of the Alps. The most important of these is undoubtedly **Oropa**. This 'Sacro Monte', dedicated to the Virgin Mary, is situated in a wide Alpine valley and comprises 12 chapels scattered throughout the woods which cover the mountain slopes. Some of these chapels contain wonderful statues by **Giovanni d'Enrico**, an artist from Val Sesia who also worked at the Varallo 'Sacro Monte'. The '**Sacro Monte**' of **Graglia** dates from the 17th century but remained unfinished and comprises only 5 chapels. The shrine at **Andorno** has 9 chapels and is also 17th century.

Cuneo, 'Granda Province'

Saluzzo with a backdrop of Monviso. A charming town, it is strategically situated to visit many other interesting places.

CUNEO AND ITS PROVINCE

*Cuneo was founded in 1198 on a plateau encircled by
the Maritime Alps by a group of people who refused to
pay taxes imposed by the Marquis of Saluzzo.
The city subsequently became a 'libero comune',
an independent municipality.*

Its name is derived from the wedge-shaped piece of land it was
built on ('cuneo' means wedge in Italian). The town became
part of the Sabauda territories in 1382 thereby sharing the
history of this dynasty, including several sieges, the most
important of which was during Napoleonic times. Cuneo also
played an essential role in the Partisan movement during the
2nd World War.

The town's most notable monument is the **church of San
Francesco**, a 13th century Gothic building, which subsequently
underwent extensive rebuilding. The **civic museum** is housed
in the ex-convent and exhibits include a Roman lapidary,
archeological remains from prehistoric times to the Middle
Ages, works of art from the 16th and 17th centuries, (including
an altar predella by Defendente Ferrari), others from the 19th
and 20th centuries and objects of cultural and ethnic interest,
such as costumes from the Alpine valleys and agricultural
implements.

Worth a visit is the Casa-Museo Galimberti, the **house of
the Galimberti family preserved as a museum**. This late
19th century house contains paintings, sculptures and a large
library and relates the story of the lawyer Tancredi and his son,
Duccio, hero of the Resistance in the area and killed in 1944.

The province of Cuneo is the largest in Piedmont, and is
known in fact as 'Provincia Granda', or 'big province'. This
province is dominated by its mountains, the highest of which is
Mon Viso at 3841m. There are many places of historical and
artistic interest for the tourist to enjoy.

Saluzzo was, from 1142 to 1601, capital of a small independent marquisate of the larger dukedom of Sabauda. After this
date, it became part of the Sabauda territories. A lovely little
town, it still displays evidence of its prestigious past. A walk
around its 'centro storico' should start from the elegantly
Provencal-Gothic **cathedral**, which contains works by the
Renaissance artist **Hans Clemer**, once known as **Maestro**

d'Elva for the wonderful cycle of frescoes he painted in the church of Elva high in the mountains. The **Museo Casa Cavassa**, a museum set in a 15th century nobleman's house, also possesses frescoes by Clemer, dated to the beginning of the 16th century. In addition, the museum contains Clemer's famous Madonna della Misericordia. Nearby is the medieval **church of San Giovanni**.

In close proximity to Saluzzo, the **castle of Manta** possesses an extraordinary cycle of frescoes in its banqueting hall which depict the **fountain of eternal youth together with maidens and cavaliers**. At Revello, also nearby, the **Cappella Marchionale** can be admired, a late gothic church containing frescoes possibly by Clemer and a Last Supper, dated 1512 and clearly inspired by Leonardo's great work in Milan.

The **abbey of Staffarda** is a splendid complex built during the 12th and 13th centuries. Here, it is possible to visit the cloisters, lodge and the church, of great architectural interest, which displays fascinating works of art.

The town of **Savigliano** is of interest for its **civic museum 'Antonino Olmo'** which contains an archeological section, an art gallery and a museum of plaster statues, the **Gipsoteca Davide Calandra**, renowned Piedmontese artist.

Fossano is famous for its impressive 14th century castle, once the home of King Emanuele Filiberto of Savoy and, subsequently, his son Carlo Emanuele I. Several of the rooms contain frescoes and the castle also houses the civic library as well as conference halls.

Mondovì is divided into 2 parts: the upper part, called *'Piazza'* is high on a hill and worth visiting for its attractive medieval buildings. Its Jesuit church, known as **La Missione**, the mission, was built by Giovenale Boetto in the 17th century and contains frescoes by Andrea Pozzo, a Baroque master. Many of the churches and chapels to be found in and around Mondovì are decorated with 15th century frescoes.

Near Mondovì is the sanctuary of **Vicoforte**, which dates from 1596. Other towns of primary importance as far as wine and food tourism are concerned are Alba and Bra, of which more will be mentioned in the following chapters.

Frescoes in the castle of Manta near Saluzzo.

The Abbey of Staffarda.

NOVARA AND ITS PROVINCE

Novara is Piedmont's second largest town for number of inhabitants.

It is situated in the eastern part of the region not far from Lombardy and is an important industrial and commercial centre, although it too possesses an interesting historical and artistic patrimony.

The **Broletto** is a complex of 4 medieval buildings one of which houses the **civic museum**, with its many archeological and medieval artifacts, 15th century frescoes and works of art from the 16th to the 18th centuries. Here, **the gallery of modern art** is also to be found. Opposite the cathedral is the **baptistery**, dating probably from the 5th century, although it has undergone extensive rebuilding through the ages. The cathedral itself was rebuilt in the late 19th century by Alessandro Antonelli over the ruins of the preceding Romanesque one, of which only the steeple remains. Within the cathedral, works by Gaudenzio Ferrari, Bernardino Lanino and Lombard painters of the 17th century can be admired.

The town's most impressive church is without doubt **San Gaudenzio** built during the 16th and 17th centuries. Antonelli designed the cupola which dominates the town's skyline and within the church can be seen the famous painting by **Tanzio da Varallo** depicting the battle of Sennachib.

A visit to the town of **Orta** and its beautiful blue lake is a must. On the lake's **island of San Giulio** is a church containing an 11th century pulpit and works of art from various periods. The island's **'Sacro Monte'** appears to be suspended above the lake and comprises 20 chapels built mainly during the 17 century and containing magnificent statues by Cristoforo Prestinari, Dionigi Bussola and Beretta plus frescoes by Fiamminghini, Morazzone, Nuvolone and Legnanino which together create a wonderful atmosphere. **San Nazzaro di Sesia** boasts an abbey founded by the bishop of Novara Riprando in 1040, and, although it was almost completely rebuilt during the 15th century, the original lay-out is visible as is the steeple. There are 15th century frescoes to be seen inside the church and its cloisters.

◄ *The cupola of Novara's great Basilica of San Gaudenzio, symbol of the city, built by the architect A. Antonelli.*

◄ *Broletto, the city's most ancient monument, full of 15th century frescoes, paintings from the 16th, 17th and 18th centuries and archaeological exhibits from the Middle Ages.*

VERCELLI AND ITS PROVINCE

*O*nce belonging to the Visconti family, Vercelli was ceded to the Savoys in 1427. It was a member of the Viscontis, Matteo, who built the **castle** in 1290 which subsequently became home to the dukes of Savoy and, after extensive rebuilding, now houses the courtroom.

The **Basilica di Sant'Andrea** is a 12th to 13th century church of exceptional interest, one of the most impressive of its kind in the Padana region. The great medieval architect and sculptor Benedetto Antelami probably worked on its construction. Noteworthy is also the 16th century **church of San Cristoforo** the inside of which is decorated with marvellous frescoes by Gaudenzio Ferrari, Val Sesia's great painter (circa 1471 to 1546).

Vercelli's centro storico is one of Piedmont's finest. Among the palaces worth a mention are: **Palazzo Alciati**, built during the 15th to 16th centuries which contains some lovely frescoes and **Palazzo Tizzoni** which also contains frescoes on a profane theme by Guglielmo Caccia ('Moncalvo'). **Palazzo Centori** is a lovely example of a Renaissance residence with its gracious Lombard-style courtyard decorated with frescoes. The Alciati residence and the nearby **Palazzo Langosco** house the **Museo Camillo Leone** collection with archeological remains from the Paleolithic to Roman times in addition to a collection of paintings and objet d'art.

The **Francesco Borgogna museum** is one of the finest art galleries in the region. Here, works by Piedmontese artists from the 15th to the 18th centuries are displayed plus an interesting collection of other Italian and foreign masters. Most of these works were donated to the city by the lawyer Antonio Borgogna in 1907.

Vercelli province is famous for its rice paddies which dominate the landscape. However, it also boasts a stupendous, if limited, stretch of Alps which includes one of the highest and most glorious peaks in Europe, **Monte Rosa**. At its feet lies **Varallo Sesia**, the valley's main town. Varallo was probably founded in pre-Roman times. During the 15th century it became part of the dukedom of Milan while maintaining a certain degree of independence and privilege and in the 17th century it was incorporated into the Sabauda dukedom. Among its features of interest are the **civic art gallery** which displays a large

The cathedral of Sant'Andrea with its cloisters

The figures of the 'Sacri Monti', the 'Sacred Mounts', represent the society of their times as seen and interpreted by the artist. Varallo, the oldest of the Piedmontese and Lombard "Sacri Monti" is exemplary in this respect.
Here, the costumes, gestures and expressions of times past can be observed as children and animals intermingle with biblical subjects.

collection of Piedmontese works, from Gaudenzio Ferrari and Tanzio da Varallo to artists of the 19th century.

The most famous tourist attraction is the '**Sacro Monte**', the oldest of all in the regions of Piedmont and Lombardy, and on which all others were based. It was constructed towards the end of the 15th century by Father Bernardino Caimi who, on his return from Palestine, wanted to recreate the atmosphere of a pilgrim's progress around Jerusalem through a series of chapels situated in the woods. He engaged Gaudenzio Ferrari to work on the paintings and sculptures. Saint Carlo Borromeo further developed the shrine during the 17th century with the works of other great artists such as Tanzio da Varallo and his brother Giovanni d'Enrico. Today, 43 chapels of great artistic value can still be visited throughout the woods in an atmosphere of touchingly sincere popular faith.

Also to be visited in Val Sesia are the typical houses of the **Walser** population which inhabit the high valley area around **Alagna**. The **National Park of Lame di Sesia** is divided between the provinces of Vercelli and Novara and contains marshland interspersed with small lakes formed by loops of the river Sesia.

*A much-awarded 'trifolao', truffle hunter,
and his beloved dog share a repast*

TREASURES OF THE EARTH

TRUFFLES
HAZELNUTS
WILD MUSHROOMS
CHESTNUTS
PEPPERS
THE LEEK OF CERVERE
THE CARDOON OF NIZZA
RICE
HONEY
FRUIT

*P*iedmont is an area which produces many delights
for the palate. In this fertile region, dozens of varieties of
fruit, vegetables and cereal crops are cultivated
to the highest level of quality.

Who doesn't immediately think of Alba when the aroma of
white truffle comes to mind? Not to mention the irresistible flavour of hazelnuts from Cortemilia or that of Cuneo's unique
wild mushrooms and marron chestnuts...

Once you've tried Nizza's cardoons, Cervere's leeks and peppers from Carmagnola, you won't want to eat vegetables from
anywhere else! Piedmont is renowned for its strawberries from
Sommariva Perno, cherries, peaches from Canale, Madernassa
pears and plums from the Roero area, Saluzzo apples and apricots from the Val Varaita.

Vercelli is the home of Italian 'risotto' rice. As you drive through Piedmont, from north to south, you can't help but be struck
by the immense rice paddies stretching over the plain, where
varieties such as Carnaroli, Arborio, Vialone and Roma are cultivated.

On the following pages you will find some interesting and
curious facts about Piedmont's gems of the earth.

*S*oil-type is at the basis of the excellence of any agricultural
product, including the great wines and truffles typical of Piedmont.

THE TRUFFLE

The truffle possesses an aroma able to inebriate man: this is the feature of its treasure that Alba likes to emphasise, over and above any scientific classification or mycological study. Certainly, this is the most noble of all mushrooms and the most mysterious of all the earth's fruits, as well as being the most exciting of all the taste sensations that the Langa and Roero area have to offer.

Truffle hunting is a pleasure but also an art, growing out of the relationship between the truffle hunter, or 'trifolao' in local dialect, and his dog. Truffles grow close to the roots of certain trees - ancient oaks, florid limes, poplars hidden away in forgotten valleys and little willows. The trifolao goes hunting at night: 'to let the dogs work undisturbed' you will hear him explain, although the truth is that darkness hides the trifolao's jealously guarded secret, that of the whereabouts of the most fruitful trees. The most perfumed or biggest truffles, sometimes weighing up to 1 kg each, are always found beneath the same trees and usually on the same day of the year. It is this that calls the trifolao out into the woods in the pitch-black of night.

Interest in the truffle goes back a long time. The Romans believed they were formed after lightning sent by Jove had struck an oak tree, symbol of strength. This curious combination produced the truffle which possessed singular powers to enhance fertility. In fact, Jove used the truffle to seduce both goddesses and terrestrial women who were unable to resist its intoxicating perfume. Jove was right- scientific analysis has shown that the white truffle of Alba probably contains pheromones, substances which can render food truly aphrodisiac.

In any case, the Romans enjoyed truffles in large quantities and they turn up in Latin literature. One of the 'tastiest' is in a tract by Apicio, who edited a sort of Ancient Roman recipe book. It is known that the Romans did not use the truffle raw, as we do, but liked to cook it beneath hot ashes and use it as a side dish. Times have changed but the truffle remains. Today we prefer to slice it very finely over piping hot , simple dishes in order to enhance its perfume to a maximum. Typical dishes suitable for truffle are poached egg, fondue, white rice and 'tajarin', or egg noodles. Just a few grams of the aromatic fungus are enough to transform these dishes into an extraordinary experience.

What does a truffle smell of? The best possess an aroma of garlic with notes of hay and honey and a whiff of spices. Studies demonstrate that the truffle's perfume, despite being one of the most complex in the whole of gastronomy is also unique to each and every truffle and can even change from day to day. Alba's truffles must be consumed when fresh and are not suitable for storing. This is the only way to truly appreciate Alba's amazing gift of nature.

Hazelnuts

*P*iedmont's hazels are grown in the Alta Langa hill region and belong to the variety 'Tonda Gentile delle Langhe'. Since 1993 these nuts grow in an area designated 'IGP' or 'Indicazione Geografica Protetta' (protected geographical area) by the Ministry of Agriculture which these days is more extensive than in the past.

Piedmont alone produces around 2% of total world hazel production and this variety is renowned for its high quality and production and excellent flavour. For this reason, all major producers of chocolate, biscuits and so on use these nuts in their recipes. During the past few years, its high quality plus some exceptionally low-yielding harvests have led to an increase in price of over 50% for this variety compared to others.

This hazel may be recognised by its round shape and high mass of fruit compared to shell (about 40 - 50% fruit against the 30 - 35% of other varieties) and also by the ease with which it is skinned after toasting. Harvest time is variable, depending on the climate, but usually occurs either in August or September. Gathering commences once the nuts have started to drop and, despite recent technology which has consented most nuts to be harvested mechanically, around 20% must still be gathered by hand.

Pietro Ferrero's world - famous Nutella, invented in Alba just after the 2nd World War, gave the hazel industry an immense boost. These days, thanks to the imagination and creativity of local chefs, the hazel is also used in many savoury dishes, including starters and meat courses. In the past, especially during the post-war period, toasted hazels were used by poorer families instead of coffee to make 'espresso'. Even the shells are utilised in the production of some pharmaceutical products or as fuel in special burners for central-heating.

*A 'hazelnut fact':
the symbol of the international
medical community includes both a cross
and a hazel branch, in recognition
of its medicinal properties.*

WILD MUSHROOMS

Unspoilt woods,
a favourable climate and earth rich in mineral
elements facilitate the growth of mushrooms and
Piedmont has them all.

The best-known variety of edible wild mushroom is certainly the 'porcino' or *Boletus Edulis*, with its intense perfume and unbeatable flavour.

These mushrooms grow during the hot months at the feet of oaks and chestnut trees and are identified by the nut-brown colour of their cap with a lighter-coloured underside and stalk. They may be consumed uncooked as a salad with an olive oil and lemon juice dressing, fried with garlic, oil and chopped parsley or deep-fried in batter. They can also be dried for storing or bottled under oil and, indeed, there are many small family firms in Piedmont who sell products prepared in this way.

Another variety found in the area and excellent both in salads or dressed with flakes of truffle, is the 'ovulo' or 'egg', (*Amanita Caesarea*). This mushroom, in its first stage of development, really does resemble an egg although later it forms a red cap with a yellowish stalk.

Other edible mushrooms which may be found in Piedmont are 'chiodino' or 'nail', 'gallinaccio', 'spugnola' or 'sponge' and 'garitula'.

Mushroom gathering is regulated by laws which indicate the time of year, area and quantity permitted. A permit can be acquired from town halls or 'comunità montana' organisations.

The best woods for mushrooming are to be found in the Ceva and Mondovì areas and also in Val Sesia, the area btween Acqui and Sassello, the Bormida and Uzzone valleys and around the comunes of Pezzolo, Castelletto and Perletto in the Alta Langa area. In the past, these mushrooms which today we can enjoy in delicious dishes of all sorts, were considered humble fare and were collected and stored by the poor for a rainy day.

The art of mushrooming helped to keep undergrowth at bay in the woods and inspired many stories and legends.

CHESTNUTS

The same favourable climate,
woods and terrain that produce mushrooms also explain
why in Piedmont such excellent chestnuts grow.

In fact, the chestnut tree is ubiquitous in the Alpine valleys and its fruit is of exceptionally high quality. There are several varieties which differ in flavour and consistency: some types are ideal for making chestnut flour, others for eating fresh and yet others for cakes and biscuits. The famous Garroni and Marroni di Chiusa Pesio varieties are found in the Stura, Gesso, Pesio and Vermenagna valleys around Cuneo and in 1992 these were awarded the IGP (Indicazione Geografica Protetta) in recognition of their superior quality.

Chestnuts were once a vital part of the staple diet of the valley folk. They would be cooked in milk, dried or ground up into flour and used to prepare polenta, bread and soup to name but a few of the dishes. In fact, from a nutritional point of view, chestnuts are rich in fibre, sugars, vitamins, minerals and essential amino acids.

Modern cuisine still uses chestnuts in a wide variety of dishes, such as homemade pasta and both white and red roast meats. Most of the Marroni chestnuts are made into marron glacé and exported. The wood of the chestnut tree is prized for the production of furniture.

Chestnut leaves once were used in the making of mattresses which, as well as being economical, were reputed to have medicinal properties. A museum of the chestnut is open to the public in Boves.

A 'scau', ancient drying-house for chestnuts.

PEPPERS

*Peppers were first cultivated
in Piedmont during the 1930s with a strain
known as 'Cuneo', rather square in shape.*

The areas particularly suited to the growing of peppers are to found around Carmagnola, near Turin, and also in Ceresole d'Alba and Sommariva Bosco and in Motta di Costigliole between Alba and Asti.

Peppers were once grown in the open field and harvesting was thus restricted to the summer or early autumn. These days, the use of green houses has meant that they can be grown practically all year round. Piedmontese peppers are distinguished by their red or yellow colour, at times streaked with green and their considerable size. The flesh is abundant and the flavour round, making them particularly suitable for the canning industry.

Peppers are protagonists of Piedmontese cuisine as an essential part of 'Bagna Cauda' and are also used in soups and red and white meat dishes.

THE CERVERE LEEK

The leek is grown in the area around both Alba and Bra, the centre of cultivation being Cervere, a few kilometres from the latter.

Here, the sandy terrain is ideal for the leek and the variety most grown is known as 'porro lungo di Cervere', or 'the long leek of Cervere'. Its distinguishing characteristics are a slender stalk, a high percentage of tender white flesh and a round flavour.

The major growers have founded a consortium for the safeguarding of their leek. The harvest begins at the end of October. The leek is used in the preparation of starters in tasty flans, in main dishes such as risotto and in homemade pasta.

RICE

*Usually when we think of rice faraway places
spring to mind, such as China,
Thailand or South America.
Piedmont, although not all are aware of this fact,
has a long history of rice-growing and the quality
varieties Arborio, Carnaroli, Vialone and Roma have
long been cultivated there.
The north-eastern part of the region,
with Vercelli as its main town is the biggest producer
although rice is also grown around Novara.*

Rice was introduced into Italy in the 12th century. Today it plays an essential role in Piedmontese economy and is an important competitor on the European and world markets.

For an Italian, the cultivation of rice brings to mind an image of toil, poverty and emigration in a harsh environment. The 'mondine', the women who emigrated to the area to work in the paddies became a symbol of this, as they worked bent double, to weed the fields of rice beneath their wide-brimmed hats. This world came to an end with the advent of modern technology but remains a potent memory. The film 'Riso Amaro' (1949) directed by the unforgettable Giuseppe De Santis portrayed the life and times of these courageous women in a direct, even crude way through a wonderful performance by the actress Silvana Mangano. Rice also symbolises the astute industriousness of the Piedmontese people.

It was towards the end of the 19th century that Count Camillo Benso, Prime Minister of the Kingdom of Italy at the time, designed the 'Cavour channels', irrigation ditches which could supply water to the fields in a time of expansion of this type of cultivation. These ditches, which carry water from the Po river, are still in use today.

Today's cuisine makes good use of rice in many forms. Risotto al Barolo, with Gorgonzola, with Castelmagno cheese, with hazelnuts or 'torta di riso', savoury rice cake, are but a few of these dishes and can be found on any excellent restaurant's menu.

For the tourist interested in visiting a typical rice farm or even in 'rice tasting', there are many such farms which will welcome you in, especially around the Vercelli region.

FOR INFORMATION CONTACT:
Ecori, Via Carlo I° di Savoia, 2 - 13100 Vercelli (VC)
Telephone: 0161 502034

THE CARDOON OF NIZZA MONFERRATO

This unique and mysterious vegetable was imported into the Nizza Monferrato area from North Africa about half way through the 19th century.

An ideal terrain and microclimate for its cultivation are to be found on the river Belbo floodlands around the Nizza Monferrato area. Only a very few farmers lavish their labours on this vegetable owing to lack of suitable land. The typically bitter flavour of the cardoon is mitigated in the Nizza variety by the presence of a chlorophyll variant. The variety is also more tender than other types of cardoon and can even be consumed raw. The cardoon belongs to the artichoke family and is unusual in that it does not require either irrigation or fertiliser and can be considered an entirely organic product.

The cardoon is sown in the spring and matures towards the end of September. After this period, when varieties from other parts of the world have already appeared on the market, the Nizza cardoon is carefully treated in the following manner: the leaves are buried about 15 cm beneath the earth to prevent them freezing and growth continues in this way ensuring that the vegetable assumes its characteristic 'hunch-backed' appearance and develops its delicate flavour. It is for this reason that the Nizza cardoon, after such careful nursing, is so superior to other varieties.

This cardoon cannot be exported owing to its tendency to precocious oxidation, even though this does not corrupt the flavour. There are only about a dozen producers who dedicate themselves to the cultivation of the Nizza cardoon and they have formed an association to promote interest in this vegetable and to protect its production, requesting DOP certification ('Denominazione di Origine Protetta', or protected zone of origin).

HONEY

*Piedmontese honey, although of very high quality and excellent flavour,
is one of the region's lesser-known products.
In fact, Piedmont possesses the qualities - pure air,
variety of flowers and uncontaminated countryside -
necessary for honey of the highest order.*

Varieties produced in the region are acacia flower, chestnut flower, orange flower, mixed flowers and cherry blossom.

Montezemolo is one of the main areas of production. This village is situated in the province of Cuneo among the hills which surround the town of Ceva, on the border with the region of Liguria. Here, on the edge of the Belbo Natural Park, an annual honey fair takes place every year with various events, including a market, seminars on aspects of honey and folklore- related events.

The nuns of the congregation of the Figlie della Madre di Gesù (daughters of the Mother of Jesus) produce and sell a special mixture of honey and Aloe Vera, following a recipe given to them by the Brazilian Father Romano Zago, said to have amazing healing properties. They can be contacted at their convent in Regione Todocco in the village of Pezzolo Valle Uzzone.

FOR INFORMATION:
Comune di Montezemolo (CN) Via Padre G. Secco
Telephone: 0174 781306

FRUIT

𝒫iedmont, like many other agricultural areas, boasts a vast range of fruits, many of which are of exceptional quality.

In addition, it is often possible to buy fruit directly from the farmer himself or at one of the weekly markets which are so much a feature of the region's towns and villages.

Sommariva Perno's strawberries have recently made a comeback after a time of crisis and are now being grown in large quantities. They are grown all over the Roero area and are famous for their tasty, firm flesh and intense perfume.

Peaches have been grown around **Canale** ever since Roman times. There are 3 main varieties: those with yellow flesh, the most well-known, those with white flesh and nectarines. Peaches ripen during the summer months and are exported all over the world.

Madernassa pears are grown exclusively in the **Roero** area. They ripen in the autumn and are used to prepare a typical desert of pears caramelised in wine. The local speciality 'Mostarda d'Uva', a kind of fruit compote, also called 'Cugnà', also contains these pears. Cugnà is eaten with mature cheeses. Other varieties of pear are also grown on the gently rolling hills of Piedmont.

Kiwis, or Actinidia, a native of New Zealand, are cultivated in certain areas of Piedmont. Kiwis contain large amounts of vitamin C and are also used for medicinal purposes. At the present time, Italy is the world's major producer of this fruit and Piedmont the highest-producing region.

Other fruits which deserve a mention include apples, plums and apricots.

ornie, *typical jars containing fruit and vegetables for consumption during the winter plus tomato paste made with the last tomatoes of August.*

Where to buy typical produce

Every Piedmontese town or village has something special to offer, something to buy from its producers and farmers or from local shops. The following can only give an idea of the produce available.

- Truffles
  Tartufi Morra , Piazza Pertinace 3, 12051, Alba CN
  Telephone: 0173 290072
  Tartufi Inaudi, Via Vittorio Emanuele 23/a, 12051, Alba CN
  Telephone: 0173 440166
  Tartufi Ponzio, Via Vittorio Emanuele 26, 12051, Alba, CN
  Telephone: 0173 440456

- Hazelnuts
  Pasticceria Barroero, Via Viarascio 35, 12074, Cortemilia, CN
  Telephone: 0173 821250
  Pasticceria Cane, Via Alfieri 88, 12074, Cortemilia, CN
  Telephone: 0173 81078
  Pasticceria Canobbio, Piazza O. Molinari 30, 12074, Cortemilia, CN
  Telephone: 0173 81262
  Pasticceria Cerrato, Piazza della Chiesa 2, 12070, Castelletto Uzzone, CN
  Telephone: 0173 89124
  Pasticceria Francesetti, Viale Marconi 27, 12074, Cortemilia, CN
  Telephone: 0173 81417

- Chestnuts
  Agrimontana, Località Ponte del Sale, 12011, Borgo San Dalmazzo, CN
  Telephone: 0171 261157

- Wild Mushrooms
  Carlotto Massimo, Via Reg. Piana 22, 12073, Ceva, CN
  Telephone: 0174 701237
  Olivero Funghi, Via Carducci 14, 15011, Acqui Terme AL
  Telephone: 0144 322558

- Honey
  Figlie della Madre di Gesù, regione Todocco, Pezzolo Valle Uzzone, CN
  Telephone: 0173 87002

Azienda Agricola Dotta Murialdo, Via Villa 21, 12072, Gottasecca, CN
Telephone: 0174 96026
Innamorato Alessandro, Via Cassinasco 19, 14053, Canelli, AT
Telephone: 0141 822571
Azienda Agricola Pellerino Vincenzo, Via Doglio 8, 12074, Cortemilia, CN
Telephone: 0173 81421

- *Rice*
  Tenuta Castello, Piazza Castello 8, Desana, VC
  Telephone: 0161 253352

- *Meats and Salami*
  Cooperativa Macello Sociale Valle Bormida, Via Vittorio Emanuele 12069, Saliceto, CN
  Telephone: 0174 98238
  Fungo Carni, Via Roma 90, 14043, Castello d'Annone AT
  Telephone: 0141 401696
  Carni Vallebelbo, Via San Bovo 80, 12054, Cossano Belbo, CN
  Telephone: 0141 88595

- *Typical Products in General*
  Antichi Sapori di Langa, Località Fontane 14, 12070, Torre Bormida, CN
  Telephone: 0173 88161
  Cose Buone di Campagna, Via Serra 21/c, 12050 Castagnito, CN
  Telephone: 0173 211890
  Drogheria Carosso, Via Vittorio Emanuele 23, 12051, Alba, CN
  Telephone: 0173 440600

The geometrical design of vine rows in a Langa vineyard.

GRAPES AND WINES

NEBBIOLO
BARBERA
DOLCETTO
RED WINES
WHITE WINES
GRAPPA
WINE SHOPS IN PIEDMONT
WOMEN WINE PRODUCERS

WINE

*hanks to its geological, geographical
and climactic characteristics, Piedmont is a producer
of high-quality wines on a world scale.*

Vines are mostly cultivated over the region's hills (about 30%
of the entire region at an average of 350m above sea-level). The
altitude guarantees cooler temperatures and breezes even during
the hottest summers with pronounced differences between day
and night -time temperatures. This allows grapes to ripen while
still preserving the correct level of acidity necessary for the development of body and structure.

The vineyards grow on a particularly fertile terrain composed
of crumbly rocks such as marl and arenaceous and chalky earth.
The vine has been cultivated in Piedmont since the 6th to 5th century BC, but it was during Roman times that studied methodo-
logy began to be applied to its cultivation. However, it was
during the 18th century under the house of Savoy that true evo-
lution of Piedmont's wines could occur with development of techniques of cultivation and the first exclusive zones.

Contrary to other wine-growing regions of the world,
Piedmont's varietals do not produce the same results if cultivated elsewhere. This is due to the characteristics of the earth and
microclimate of the Piedmontese hills. Nebbiolo, Barbera,
Dolcetto, Cortese and Moscato are just not the same thing at all
if grown in another place - they are uniquely Piedmontese.

It should be noted that over 40% of wine produced in Piedmont
is DOC ('Denominazione di Origine Controllata' or controlled
zone of origin) or DOCG ('Denominazione di Origine
Controllata e Garantita' or controlled and guaranteed zone of
origin). In fact, Piedmont is second only to the Veneto region in
Italy for quantity of quality wine produced, taking precedent over
Tuscany.

The areas of most intensive vine cultivation are to be found in
the south of the region, in the Alba and Langhe areas plus those

A vineyard just before the harvest is a heart-lifting sight.

Autumn arrives in the Langa perfumed with the scents of wine and truffles

of Bra, Asti, Alessandria and Monferrato. Other areas which need mentioning are those around Turin, Novara and Vercelli. Alba and the Langhe are the areas in which the great reds such as Barolo and Barbaresco are produced, taking their names from their places of origin. Other wines produced here are Barbera, Dolcetto, Nebbiolo and Moscato.

Bra and the Roero are the home of whites such as Arneis and Favorita and also, in the Roero, the reds Barbera and Birbet. In the Asti part of Monferrato it is Barbera which takes pride of place although Grignolino and Moscato, a sweet and aromatic white, must also be mentioned. The Alessandria side of Monferrato is divided into the territories of Gavi, (where the wine of the same name is produced) Acqui and Casale. Acqui is home to Brachetto, a sweet aromatic red, while Grignolino is produced in Casale.

In the province of Turin we can expect to find Carema, Freisa and Dolcetto with Erbaluce di Caluso the best-known white. The province of Vercelli is home to Gattinara and Spanna and Novara to Ghemme, Fara and Sizzano.

The following is a list of Piedmontese varietals from which some of the most famed wines are produced:

Red Wines

- **Nebbiolo** is used to produce Barolo, Barbaresco, Roero, Nebbiolo, Gattinara, Ghemme, Carema.
- **Barbera** is used for Barbera d'Alba, Barbera d'Asti, Barbera del Monferrato, Langhe Barbera and Piemonte Barbera.
- **Dolcetto** is used for Dolcetto d'Alba, Dolcetto di Diano, Dolcetto di Dogliani, Dolcetto delle Langhe Monregalesi, Dolcetto d'Asti, Dolcetto d'Acqui and Dolcetto di Ovada.
- **Brachetto** is used for Brachetto d'Acqui, Piemonte Brachetto, Birbet.
- **Grignolino** is used for Grignolino d'Asti, Grignolino del Monferrato Casalese.
- **Pelaverga** is used for Verduno Pelaverga.
- **Freisa** is used for Langhe Freisa, Freisa d'Asti.

Children proudly display their bunches of grapes in a photo of around 1895 from the Fontanafredda archives.

White Wines

- **Cortese** is used for Gavi, including the sparkling version, Cortese del Monferrato
- **Moscato** is used for the production of sweet, aromatic wines: Moscato d'Asti, Asti Spumante, Piemonte Moscato, Piemonte Moscato Passito
- **Arneis** is used for Roero Arneis, Langhe Arneis
- **Favorita** is used for Langhe Favorita
- **Erbaluce** is used for Erbaluce di Caluso in the sparkling or passito forms.

Piedmont boasts 8 DOCG wines of which 5 are reds, (Barolo, Barbaresco, Gattinara, Ghemme, Brachetto d'Acqui) and 3 whites (Moscato d'Asti, Asti Spumante and Gavi). A further 2 wines are about to be included in the list, the red Roero and the white Roero Arneis. The legal procedure for their acceptance is under way at a national level, having already passed at regional level.

In addition to these native wines, Piedmont also produces small quantities of classic wines and spumantes, including Pinot Nero, Cabernet Sauvignon, Merlot, Shiraz for the reds and Chardonnay, Sauvignon, Pinot Bianco and Riesling among the whites.

If you are a wine lover, one of the most pleasurable experiences during a holiday in Piedmont is a visit to a local winery, whether it be Barolo, Barbaresco, Moscato or any other variety. Over the next few pages, at the end of a description of each wine, you will find a list of producers, both famous and lesser known, for whom we can guarantee the excellence of both wines and hospitality. However, we do advise phoning in advance to fix an appointment.

MODULARIO
a.i./ n. 838

Mod. 1/DOCG

AAF 07175556
BAROLO
DENOMINAZIONE DI ORIGINE CONTROLLATA E GARANTITA
LITRI 0.750
I.A.Z.S. - OFF.C.V. - ROMA

A DOCG collar, printed and numbered by the Ministry for Agricultural Policies, is attached to each bottle and guarantees the wine's quality

An ancient winery.

A modern winery equipped with precision instruments for controlling every phase of the wine-making process.

A bunch of grapes on the cane seems to blend into those sculpted on a barrel in this inspired photograph.

NEBBIOLO

*The Nebbiolo vine is Piedmont's star,
producing some of the world's finest wines:
Barolo, Barbaresco,
Gattinara and Ghemme to name but some.*

It is the area's microclimate and particular soil-type which result in such spectacular wines - in no other part of the planet does this vine produce wines of similar quality. Wine producers who emigrated from Piedmont to California, Australia and South Africa have tried to cultivate it in these parts of the world but the results were never encouraging enough to persist.

Sub-varieties of Nebbiolo cultivated in Piedmont are Lampia, Michet and Rosè which are used to produce Barolo and Barbaresco. Roero, Picoutener and Carema on the other hand are used for the production of Carema and other wines in the north-east part of the region.

These grapes result in a combination of sugars, alcohol, acidity and tannins which give a long-lived wine of superb structure and elegance.

The heart of Barolo country is the area around Alba, the Langhe and the Roero. The hilly territory comprises 10 comunes, at a distance of about 10 km outside Alba. To the east of Alba, beginning at San Rocco Seno d'Elvio, is the area dedicated to Barbaresco, a total of 4 comunes.

North of Alba, in the Roero area, Nebbiolo is grown and used to produce the wine known as Roero in a total of 15 comunes. In Vercelli province, the Nebbiolo varietal is used to make Gattinara, Bramaterra and Lessone. In the province of Novara, Ghemme, Sizzano, Fara and Boca are all wines made with the varietal, taking their names from the comunes of origin. Finally, the province of Turin is home to Carema, also named after its comune.

Outside Piedmont, the Nebbiolo varietal is grown in the Valtellina area in the province of Sondrio where its sub-variety

Chiavennasca is used to make Valtellina, Sassella, Grumello, Inferno and Valgella.

The following is a list of Nebbiolo wine characteristics:

WINE	YIELD (quintals/hectare)	ALCOHOL (content)	AGEING (months)
Barolo DOCG	80	13 %	38
Barolo DOCG Res.	80	13 %	62
Roero DOC	80	11.5 %	7
Roero DOC Sup.	80	12 %	7
Nebbiolo Langhe DOC	90	11.5 %	-
Nebbiolo d'Alba DOC	90	12 %	12
Gattinara DOCG	75	12.5 %	37
Gattinara DOCG Res.	75	13 %	49
Barbaresco DOCG	80	12.5 %	26
Barbaresco DOCG Res.	80	12.5 %	48

BAROLO

Some of Barolo's defining features:

Grape:	**100% Nebbiolo**
DOC wine:	**from 1966**
DOCG wine:	**from 1980**
Total hectares cultivated:	1253
Maximum quintals grapes grown:	99833
Yield per hectare:	**80 ql - 52 hl - 6933 bottles**
Maximum yield grapes to wine:	65%
Maximum bottles produced:	7.361.000
Minimum alcohol:	13%
Minimum acidity:	5%
Minimum ageing:	**38 months or 62 months for Reserve**
Serve at:	**18° c**

The village of Barolo surrounded by vineyards and castles.

$\mathscr{B}$arolo, once called
'The wine of Kings and the King of wines'
is rightly considered one of the world's greatest wines.

Its story began in the 19th century when the Marchioness Giulia Colbert di Maulévrier, wife of the Marquis Falletti di Barolo, discovered the wine's potential. The Marchioness was French and a wine-lover and vineyards grew all around her husband's castle. Until that moment, the Barolo produced with these grapes had been vinified as a sweet wine which did not resemble the great French reds in any way, with their body, perfumes, longevity and careful production techniques.

Barolo was born from the application of French techniques of vine cultivation and wine production and its name first began to appear on labelled bottles. From that time onwards, Barolo has been appreciated on the best tables around the world. Historical documents prove how this wine was requested by ambassadors, popes, prime ministers and sovereigns for their important occasions.

In 1878, the King of Italy, Vittorio Emanuele II, planted the vineyards at Fontanafredda in Serralunga d'Alba in order to produce Barolo. The wine gained recognition first in Italy alongside Barbaresco, Brunello di Montalcino and Chianti with

$\mathscr{A}$ Roman stone tablet dating from the first century A.D inscribed to Marcus Lucretius Crestus 'Mercator Vinarius' (wine merchant). It was found at Pollenzo near Bra in 1958.

$\mathscr{T}$he Marquise Giulia Colbert.

the DOC of 1966 and successively with the DOCG in 1980.

At the present time, Barolo's homeland comprises the villages west of Alba: Barolo, Monforte, Castiglione Falletto, La Morra, Serralunga, Grinzane Cavour, Diano d'Alba, Verduno, Roddi, Cherasco and Novello. Wine legislation requires Barolo to possess certain well-defined characteristics. It has to be produced from 100% Nebbiolo grapes using only the sub-varieties of Lampia, Michet and Rosè in vineyards which have been authorised by the Cuneo Chamber of Commerce. Ageing must not be for less than 38 months of which 2 years in oak barrels or 62 months and 3 years in oak for Reserve. Maximum production in the vineyard is 80 quintals per hectare. There must be a minimum of 13% alcohol and 0.5% acidity.

In order to obtain the DOCG bottle collar, a wine has to be tested by a special official commission of experts, members of the Chamber of Commerce. It is they who will have the last word on the quality of the wine and on whether it merits the name 'Barolo'. If the wine is not considered to be quite up to Barolo standards, it is demoted to Nebbiolo DOC.

At tasting, Barolo is seen to possess a garnet-red colouring with ruby highlights when young, becoming orange as the wine ages. Its intense perfume brings fruit such as cherries and plums to mind with flower notes of wild rose, violet, geranium. Other perfumes are spices, such as vanilla, cinnamon and green pepper and sometimes also truffle and woodland undergrowth.

The wine is robust and full on the palate with a full structure. The acidity and tannins can be a bit fierce during its youth but mellow with age. It is for this reason that Barolo is usually drunk after 6 to 8 years of ageing although it can be kept up to 15 to 20 years.

Comparison with other world-class wines on an level international have led to some changes for Barolo too. For example, until some years ago, it was usual practice to vinify grapes from different vineyards together. These days, vineyards are often vinified as separate entities, or crus. Many producers emphasise this fact by adding the name of the specific vineyard to the label on the bottle especially if the cru is a prestigious one, such as Cannubi, Bussia, Brunate, Ornato, Lazzarito, Cerequio, Rocche dell'Annunziata or Ginestra. Other, more recently appreciated crus are Bricco Boschis, Arborina, Castelletto and Rionda.

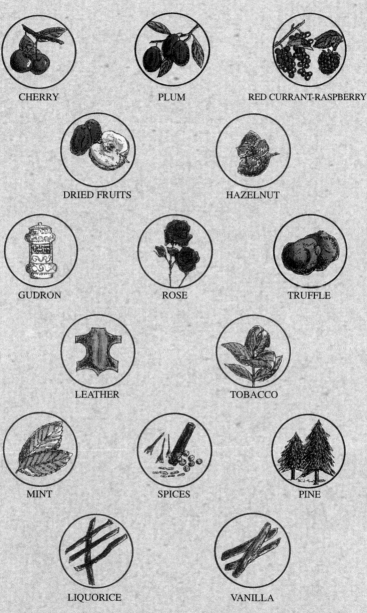

CHERRY

PLUM

RED CURRANT-RASPBERRY

DRIED FRUITS

HAZELNUT

GUDRON

ROSE

TRUFFLE

LEATHER

TOBACCO

MINT

SPICES

PINE

LIQUORICE

VANILLA

These are very long-lived wines, pleasing even after 30 or 40 years with enhancement of the 'aftertastes' depicted above.

A further positive characteristic of Barolo is the increase in number of small-scale producers since the 1960s, when there used to be only about a dozen. These days, around 150 young producers dedicate themselves to the production of Barolo on their own farms instead of the old-style method of growing the grapes and then selling them to a larger firm for production. In this way, they have control over the quality of their wine during every phase of cultivation and vinification. They personally supervise the pruning and spraying and the selection of bunches of fruit suitable for harvesting and this translates into a product of the very highest quality.

Barolo can be consumed together with dishes such as game, braised meats or matured cheese. It is a wine that can also be consumed by itself, a wine for meditation.

SOME MAIN PRODUCERS OF BAROLO:

Fratelli Cavallotto Address: Via Alba-Monforte 48, 12060, Castiglione Falletto, CN
Telephone: 0173 62914 - e-mail: info@cavallotto.com
This firm has belonged to the Cavallotto brothers since 1948 and is now run by a 5th generation of producers, making superb wines. In addition to Barolo, they also make Barbera and Dolcetto.

Prunotto Address: Località San Cassiano 4/g, 12051, Alba, CN
Telephone: 0173 280017 / 281167 - e-mail: prunotto@prunotto.it
An historical firm of Langhe producers today owned by the Antinori family. Here, Barolo, Barbaresco, Barbera d'Asti, Barbera d'Alba and Dolcetto are produced.

Pio Cesare Address: Via Cesare Balbo 6, 12051, Alba, CN
Telephone: 0173 440386 - FAX: 0173 363680
e-mail: piocesare@piocesare.it
An historical firm which has won many prizes for its wines. The winery has Roman foundations, still visible today. It produces Barolo, Barbaresco, Barbera, Dolcetto and Arneis.

Borgogno Address: Via Gioberti 1, 12060, Barolo, CN
Telephone: 0173 56108 - FAX: 0173 5634
e-mail: borgogno-barolo@libero.it
One of the oldest Barolo wineries, it was founded in 1761. Today it is run by the Boschis family, direct descendants of the founder. As well as Barolo, it produces Barolo Chinato, Dolcetto and Barbera.

Elio Grasso Address: Località Ginestra 40, 12065, Monforte d'Alba CN
Telephone: 0173 78491 - FAX: 0173 789907
e-mail: eliograsso@isiline.it
One of the newer firms, this family produces Barolo, Barbera and Dolcetto.

Marchesi di Barolo Address: Via Alba 12, 12060, Barolo, CN
Telephone: 0173 564400   FAX: 0173 56444
e-mail: marchesi.barolo@marchesibarolo.com
Barolo was born here in this historical winery during the 18th century. Barbera, Dolcetto and Moscato are also produced.

Many producers add the name of sub-zones of the various areas of production to their labels. These **sub-zones** are included on special maps.

The **comune of Barolo** has 31, for example those of Cannubi, Valletta,Fossati and Vignane.

The comune of **Castiglione Falletto** has 24, including those of Rocche, Serra, Brunella and Scarrone.

The comune of **Grinzane Cavour** has 9 including those of La Corte, Canova and Raviole.

The comune of **La Morra** has 27, including Cerequio, Brunate, Bricco Rocca and Serra dei Turchi.

The comune of **Monforte** has 10, including Bussia, Perno and Ravera.

The comune of **Novello** has 7 including Ravera, Corini-Pallaretta.

The comune of **Serralunga** has 42, including Costabella, San Rocco, Pradone, La Serra and Falletto.

The comune of **Verduno** has 12, including San Lorenzo, Massara and Riva.

BARBARESCO

Some of Barbaresco's defining features:

Grape:	100% Nebbiolo
DOC wine:	from 1966
DOCG wine:	from 1980
Hectares cultivated:	483
Maximum quintals grapes produced:	38550
Yield per hectare:	80 ql - 52 hl - 6933 bottles
Grape-wine yield:	65%
Maximum bottles produced:	2736.533
Minimum alcohol:	12.5 %
Minimum acidity:	5 °/oo
Minimum ageing:	26 months or 48 for Reserve
Serve at:	18 ° c

If Barolo is the 'King of Wines' then Barbaresco is the Queen.

It is produced exclusively with Nebbiolo grapes in a zone of production which lies within 4 hill-top villages to the east of Alba: Barbaresco, Neive, Treiso and San Rocco Seno D'Elvio in the area of Alba itself.

Barbaresco was first made by Domizio Cavazza, a lecturer from Barbaresco at the Royal Enological School of Alba. He was the first to understand the great potential of the Nebbiolo grape cultivated over the hills of his native Barbaresco. To protect the integrity of the wine he founded a co operative of Barbaresco wine producers, one of the very first of its kind in Italy. In 1933, this wine obtained the title of 'typical wine' by a special decree. It became DOC in 1966 and DOCG in 1980.

Barbaresco possesses a garnet-red colouring with ruby highlights which tend to orange as the wine ages. It has a full body and robust structure. Its perfumes, ample and ethereal, vary from flowers such as dog rose, violet and geranium to fruit such as cherry and plum jam. Spices are also present, including vanilla, cinnamon and green pepper and there is often a note of truffle.

This wine also tends to fierceness when young, maturing its acidity and tannins with age and is particularly long-lived. It is best to taste Barbaresco after 5 to 12 years of ageing although it can be kept up to 25 to 30 years. When compared to Barolo, it is often considered a more elegant and genteel wine.

Like Barolo, the Chamber of Commerce must authorise the

vineyards of Nebbiolo where it is produced. No more than 80 quintals are to be produced per hectare and the wine must be aged for a minimum of 26 months with 1 year in oak barrels, or 48 months and 2 years for Reserve. Minimum alcohol content is 12.5% with minimum acidity 0.5%.

Producers tend to vinify single vineyards for this wine too and labels will often indicate a particular cru. Some of the oldest are Rabajà, Santo Stefano, Asili, Pora and Ovello. Newer crus include Gallina, Faset and Martinenga.

Much of Barbaresco's fame is due to the work of Angelo Gaja, son of Giovanni, who was mayor of his village during the 1960s. Over the years, Gaja has brought this wine to the attention of the world's most prestigious restaurants and wine writers through admirable hard work both in the vineyard and the winery but also at a marketing and commercial level. These days, Barbaresco can take its place alongside the world's most famous wines.

Barbaresco is ideal for consumption with wild mushrooms, roasts and matured cheeses.

SOME MAIN BARBARESCO PRODUCERS:
Ca Romè
*Address: Via Rabajà 36, 12050, Barbaresco, CN
Telephone: 0173 635126   FAX: 0173 635175
Romano Marengo and his family who own this firm are as unique as is their wine. In addition to Barolo they produce Barolo, Barbera and a blended red 'Da Pruvè'.*

Fontanabianca
*Address: Via Bordini 15, 12057, Neive, CN
Telephone + FAX: 0173 67195
Founded in 1969 by Aldo Pola and Bruno Ferro, this firm is one of the best newcomers. As well as Barbaresco they produce Barbera, Dolcetto and Arneis.*

Fratelli Grasso
*Address: Via Giacosa Regione Valgrande 1/b 12050, Treiso, CN.
Telephone + FAX: 0173 638194
The Grasso brothers offer their visitors warm hospitality and excellent wines. In addition to Barbaresco they also produce Barbera, Dolcetto and Moscato.*

The hills surrounding Barbaresco, a breath-taking sight.

ROERO

*T*his is a relative newcomer to the scene. It was awarded DOC status in 1989 and is produced using 95 % to 98% Nebbiolo grapes with the possibility of adding 2%-5% Arneis. The authorised vineyards are to be found in 15 comunes of the Roero area. Among the most important are Canale, Vezza, Montaldo, Monteu and Castellinaldo.

The regulatory body allows a maximum yield of 80 quintals per hectare and a minimum alcohol content of 11.5% or 12% for Superior. The wine has to be aged for at least 7 months.

This is an easier wine to drink when compared to Barolo or Barbaresco with less evidence of tannins and acidity, allowing it to be consumed when young, although this fact penalises it as far as ageing is concerned. It is advisable to drink this wine within 3 to 4 years after production. For the Superior version ageing can continue for 6 or 7 years.

It possesses a light ruby-red colouring and its perfumes include woodland berries, cherries, flowers and spices. It is consumed with hot Piedmontese starters, egg pasta such as 'agnolotti' and white meats.

SOME MAIN PRODUCERS:

Teo Costa
Address: Via San Salvario 1, 12050, Castellinaldo CN
Telephone + FAX: 0173 213066
The brothers Marco and Roberto Costa are performing work of quality and enthusiasm in this expanding firm. In addition to Roero they also produce Barbera, Arneis, Passito d'Arneis, Favorita and Birbet.

Angelo Negro
Address: Frazione Sant'anna 1, 12040, Monteu Roero, CN
Telephone: 0173 90252   FAX: 0173 90712
e-mail: negro@negroangelo. it

This winery was founded in 1970 and is now run by its founder's son, Giovanni, a great Roero character. He also produces Arneis, Arneis Brut, Arneis Passito, Barbera and Birbet.

Matteo Correggia
Address: Case Sparse Garbinetto 124, 12043, Canale CN
Telephone: 0173 978009   FAX: 0173 959849
e-mail: matteo@matteocorreggia.com
This producer has always aimed for the highest quality in his wines. He also produces Arneis.

Estella Canziani (Milan 1887 - London 1964)
Harvest

NEBBIOLO

As well as being the name of the vine from which
the fore-mentioned wines are produced,
Nebbiolo also exists as a wine unto itself.

There are 2 sub-types, Nebbiolo d'Alba and Langhe Nebbiolo.
Nebbiolo d'Alba is produced in about 20 comunes around the
town of Alba, except those which produce either Barolo or
Barbaresco.

The maximum yield permitted is 90 quintals per hectare and
the wine must possess 12% alcohol and have been aged for at
least 12 months. This wine has a strong structure similar to its
'big brothers' and can be aged for up to 4 to 5 years.

It is best consumed with hot starters, hot vegetables with sauces, tajarin pasta and white meats. It can also be served as a
table wine.

Langhe Nebbiolo can be produced in over 90 comunes in the
province of Cuneo including those of Barolo and Barbaresco.
This wine denomination is also utilised when a Barolo or
Barbaresco do not quite meet any of their required standards.
Maximum yield is 90 quintals per hectare and alcohol is 11.5%.
There are no particular limits to ageing. It is an easy wine to
drink and should be consumed within about 2 to 3 years from
production. It is best served with starters such as 'vitello tonnato', tagliatelle al sugo and simple meat dishes.

SOME MAIN PRODUCERS:
Poderi Colla
Address: Località San Rocco Seno d'Elvio 82, 12050, Alba CN
Telephone: 0173 290148   FAX: 0173 441498
This family has a long history as wine producers and the firm is
now run by Tino and his daughter Federica. In addition to
Nebbiolo they also produce Barbaresco, Barolo, Dolcetto and
Barbera.

Ratti

Address: Frazione Annunziata 7, 12064, La Morra CN
Telephone: 0173 50185   FAX: 0173 509373
*An historical winery which also possesses a wine museum opened
by the founder Renato Ratti. In addition to Nebbiolo it also produces Barolo, Dolcetto and Barbera.*

Giuseppe Negro

Address: Località Gallina 12057, Neive CN
Telephone + FAX: 0173 677468
*Giorgio now runs this firm which was founded by his father and
produces wines of high quality. As well as his Nebbiolo 'Monsù',
he makes Barbaresco, Barbera, Dolcetto and Arneis.*

*A picture postcard from the 1950s interesting for the inclusion
of Nebbiolo in a sparkling form.*

Barbera, widely cultivated in the provinces of Asti, Alessandria, Cuneo and Turin, is also grown in northern Piedmont.

BARBERA

arbera can be counted one of the most pleasurable 'wine discoveries' of the past few decades. Now that it has completely overcome its old image of a 'supermarket' wine, it is ready to take its place in the pantheon of internationally famous wines.

This drastic improvement in image is down to one man, Giacomo Bologna from Rocchetta Tanaro who, about 10 years ago began his work on this wine. Changes in production techniques, such as low yields in the vineyard in order to concentrate sugars, acidity and perfume, plus the use of soft crushing and barrique barrels to enhance elegance and tannins, have created a wine for the finest of palates.

The Barberas produced in Piedmont are Barbera d'Asti, Barbera d'Alba and Barbera del Monferrato. Asti is considered the most suitable terrain for the cultivation of Barbera and here top quality vineyards are dedicated to Barbera rather than Nebbiolo which is less suited to the area.

The regulatory body for Barbera limits production to 90 quintals per hectare. Alcohol content is at least 12% with a minimum ageing period of 4 months. For the Superior version, alcohol content is 12,5% and ageing 14 months.

At tasting, Barbera demonstrates important structure with an intense ruby-red colouring and perfumes which vary from flowers, such as dog rose, to fruit such as plums and woodland berries or spices such as cinnamon and vanilla. Ageing lends this wine good acidity and soft tannins. This wine is ideal with 'Bagna Cauda', risottos and meat stews. It should be consumed after 5 - 7 years although a really excellent vintage will easily last from 10 to 12 years.

Barbera d'Alba is grown within numerous comunes on the hills around the town of Alba, including the Barolo and Barbaresco areas. Its regulatory body indicates a limit of 100 quintals per hectare and a minimum alcohol level of 12%. For the classic version there is no particular minimum limit to ageing. For the Superior version, ageing must be for a minimum of 12 months with a minimum alcohol content of 12.5%. It is precisely the fact that this Barbera is grown over the Barolo and Barbaresco hills that give it such a fine flavour. Such is the quality obtained that some producers willingly make space for a Barbera among their Barolo, decreasing production of the latter. This sort of Barbera reaches the same zenith of quality – and prices - as Barolo.

Barbera d'Alba is usually a lighter wine than its Asti name-sake. It possesses good body and fine structure and is ready to drink a few months after harvesting when still very fresh. It has intense perfumes of flowers, fresh fruit and spices and is ideal when served with meat starters, pasta dishes and fairly matured cheeses. Ideally, it should be consumed after 2 to 4 years' ageing.

Barbera del Monferrato is considered the easiest to drink of the family. It is cultivated throughout a vast area of the provinces of Asti and Alessandria. Unlike the other 2 Barberas, Barbera del Monferrato is allowed to contain a small percentage of other typical varieties such as Freisa, Grignolino or Dolcetto. Maximum production per hectare is 100 quintals with a minimum alcohol content of 11.5%. A feature of this wine is that it is sometimes left slightly sparkling to enhance its youthful freshness. It is ideal for light meals or the Piedmontese 'Merenda Sinoira', or 'High Tea', served with salami, omelettes and creamy cheeses. It is usually consumed during the year after harvesting.

The following is a list of Barbera wine characteristics:

BARBERA VARIETY	YIELD PER HECTARE	ALCOHOL CONTENT	AGEING
Piemonte DOC	110 ql	11%	-
Monferrato DOC	100 ql	11.5%	-
Monferrato DOC Sup.	100 ql	12.5%	14 months
d'Alba DOC	100 ql	12%	-
d'Alba DOC Sup.	100 ql	12.5%	12 months
d'Asti DOC	90 ql	12%	4 months
d'Asti DOC Sup.	90 ql	12.5%	14 months

Other Barbera varieties are: **Gabiano, Colli Tortonesi.**

SOME MAIN PRODUCERS:

BARBERA D'ASTI
Cascina Castlet
Address: Strada Castelletto 6, 14055, Costigliole d'Asti, AT
Telephone: 0141 966651   FAX: 0141 961492
e-mail: castlet@tin.it
The owner, Mariuccia Borio is an energetic and enthusiastic person who is wonderful to get to know. As well as Barbera, she produces Moscato and a blend called 'Policalpo'.

Cantina Sociale Vinchio e Vaglio
Address: Strada Provinciale 40, Regione San Pancrazio 1, 14040 Vinchio, AT
Telephone: 0141 950903   FAX: 0141 950391
A co operative winery which offers excellent value for money. Here, Grignolino, Moscato and Dolcetto del Monferrato is also produced.

Giacomo Bologna
Address: Via Roma 94, 14030 Rocchetta Tanaro AT
Telephone: 0141 644113   FAX: 0141 644584
e-mail: info@braida.it
Giacomo Bologna's Braida winery is Barbera. He also produces Brachetto d'Acqui and Grignolino.

BARBERA D'ALBA
Elio Altare
Address: Frazione Annunziata 51, 12064 La Morra CN
Telephone: 0173 50835
As well as being a great character, Elio is also considered a main figure among the new generation of the Langhe producers. He also produces Barolo and Dolcetto.

Eraldo Viberti
Address: Borgata Tetti 53, 12064, Santa Maria di La Morra CN
Telephone: 0173 50308
A fine young producer who is very aware of the quality of his wines. He also produces Barolo, Dolcetto and a blend, 'Gilat'.

Gianfranco Alessandria
Address: Località Manzoni 13, 12065, Monforte d'Alba, CN
Telephone + FAX: 0173 78576
A small winery run by its owner. He produces Barolo, Dolcetto and a blend 'L'insieme'.

DOLCETTO

$\mathscr{I}t$ could be said that
Dolcetto is the 'wine of the Piedmontese',
the one they put on their tables
every day at lunch and dinner.

Despite its name, it is not a sweet wine but a dry one, plea-santly fruity with less body than Nebbiolo or Barbera, which can be served during any meal. It can be cultivated on any type of soil.

There are many types of Dolcetto, one for nearly every different valley. There is Dolcetto d'Alba and Dolcetto d'Asti, one from Ovada and one from Acqui, Dolcetto di Diano, Dolcetto di Dogliani, Dolcetto delle Langhe, Dolcetto Langhe Monregalesi and Piemonte Dolcetto. Each of these can be distinguished from the others by its perfumes, structure and body.

Dolcetto possesses a ruby-red colouring which varies in inten-sity according to the variety. Its fragrant, winy perfumes contain notes of fresh red fruits and almonds. The Dolcettos from Diano and Dogliani usually possess a bigger structure than the others, with a wide variety of perfumes and a pleasant freshness. Minimum alcohol content for these is 11.5% but they may pos-sess up to 13% or 14% alcohol. They are served with fairly ela-borate dishes such as fondues or wild mushroom recipes and can be aged for a few years.

The Alba, Asti and Langhe Monregalesi Dolcettos are general-ly lighter, less robust wines with less acidity. They are served with hot Piedmontese starters, salami and pasta dishes with sim-ple sauces. They are usually consumed the year following harve-st although they can be kept for 3 or 4 years.

The Acqui, Ovada, Langhe, Monferrato and Piemonte Dolcettos are, with a few exceptions, easy wines to drink with medium body and fresh perfumes. They are consumed within a year.

The following is a list of the wine's main characteristics:

VARIETY	YIELD	ALCOHOL	AGEING
	PER HECTARE	CONTENT	
Langhe DOC	100 ql	11%	-
d'Asti DOC	80 ql	11.5%	-
d'Asti DOC Sup.	80 ql	12.5%	14 months
d'Alba DOC	90 ql	11.5%	-
d'Alba DOC Sup.	90 ql	12.5%	14 months
Diano DOC	80 ql	11.5%	-
Diano DOC Sup.	80 ql	12.5%	14 months
Dogliani DOC	80 ql	11.5%	-
Dogliani DOC Sup.	80 ql	12.5%	14 months

Other varieties of Dolcetto are: **del Monferrato, di Acqui, di Ovada, delle Langhe Monregalesi.**

SOME MAIN PRODUCERS OF THE WINE ARE:

DOLCETTO D'ALBA
Flavio Roddolo Address: Località Sant'Anna 5, 12065, Monforte d'Alba CN - Telephone + FAX: 0173 78535
A small winery run with great enthusiasm by Flavio where he produces excellent wines also including Barolo and Barbera.

Fratelli Seghesio Address: Frazione Castelletto 5, 12065, Monforte d'Alba CN - Telephone + FAX: 0173 78108
Brothers Aldo and Riccardo Seghesio only started up their business in 1990 but produce excellent wines also including Barolo and Barbera.

Eredi Lodali Address: Viale Rimembranza 5, 12050, Treiso, CN Telephone: 0173 638109
A wonderfully welcoming family winery which offers great value for money. It also produces Barbaresco, Barbera and Barolo.

Diano
Gigi Rosso Address: Via Alba-Barolo 46, 12060, Castiglione Falletto CN - Telephone: 0173 262369   FAX: 0173 262224
e-mail: info@gigirosso.com
Gigi Rosso is a Patriarch of Barolo, famed also for his Dolcetto.

Bricco Maiolica Address: Via Bolangino 7, 12055, Ricca di Diano d'Alba, CN - Telephone: 0173 612049 - FAX: 0173 612549
e-mail: accomo@briccomaiolica.it

Angelo and Beppe Accomo run this winery with great enthusiasm. Their Diano is a reference point for the area. They also produce Barbera.

Claudio Alario *Address: Via Santa Croce 23, 12055, Diano d'Alba CN - Telephone: 0173 231808   FAX: 0173 231433*
Claudio, owner-enologist of this small winery has produced excellent wines here for years. He also produces Barolo, Barbera and Nebbiolo.

Dogliani
Fratelli Abbona *Address: Via Torino 242, 12063, Dogliani CN Telephone + FAX: 0173 721317*
An excellent winery which has expanded over the years and reached very high levels. It also produces Barolo, Barbaresco, Barbera and Arneis.

Annamaria Abbona *Address: Frazione Moncucco 21, 12060, Farigliano CN - Telephone + FAX: 0173 797228*
In no time at all, Annamaria's Dolcetto has reached excellence and is considered among the finest of its kind. She also produces a blend called Cadò.

Cà Viola *Address: Borgata San Luigi 11, 12063, Dogliani, CN Telephone: 0173 617013   FAX: 0173 617935*
Giuseppe Caviola is one of the country's finest enologists and his wines follow suit. He also produces a blend called Bric du Luv.

DOLCETTO D'ACQUI
Cascina Bertolotto di Traversa *Address: Via P. Porro 36, 15018, Spigno Monferrato AL*
Telephone: 0144 91223   FAX: 0144 91223
e-mail: www.poderitraversavini.it.com
Here, among the less famous hills, father Giuseppe and his children Fabio and Maria produce excellent wines served with great hospitality. They also produce Brachetto, Moscato and Barbera.

Giacomo Cavallero *Address: Regione Cavallero 102, 12059 Vesime AT - Telephone: 0144 89054*
A family-run winery very aware of quality and traditions. They also produce Cortese, Barbera and Moscato di Ovada.

DOLCETTO DEI TERRAZZAMENTI

This wine, still virtually unknown to the public, deserves a mention for the historical and cultural values it represents.

In fact, it is wine which was 'reborn' during the year 2000 thanks to the work of a group of young producers and farmers of the <u>Cortemilia area of the Bormida valley</u>.

The stone - terraced hills around the river Bormida were, until a few decades ago, covered in mainly Dolcetto-producing vineyards. The depopulation of the countryside and the low profitability of the vineyards led to them being almost completely abandoned. A group of young farmers with a particular interest in the vineyards once worked by their fathers and grandfathers utilised funds from local organisations to bring them back to working life. The creation of an 'Eco-museum' dedicated to the terraces has also helped the endeavour. The wine has been proudly named 'Langhe Dolcetto dei Terrazzamenti' or Langhe Dolcetto of the terraces.

This wine is easy to drink with a medium body and moderate alcohol content. It possesses fresh fruit and flower perfumes and is served with starters and Piedmontese pasta dishes. It is a wine for drinking young.

SOME OF THE MAIN PRODUCERS:
- **Canonica Cesare**
  Address: Via U. Maddalena 10, 12070, Torre Bormida CN
  Telephone + FAX: 0173 88026

- **Chinazzo Marco, Cascina Besciolo**
  Address: Frazione Pianelle, 12070 Gorzegno CN
  Telephone: 0173 86038

- **Fratelli Cigliutti**
  Address: Piazza Savona 22, 12074, Cortemilia CN
  Telephone: 0173 81785

- **Rossello Casa Vinicola**
  Address: Via Bergolo 10, 12074, Cortemilia, CN
  Telephone: 0173 81844

A typically beautiful image of hill terraces.

BRACHETTO

Brachetto d'Acqui was one of the last Piedmontese wines to obtain the DOCG status.
It is a sweet wine produced from red grapes, pleasantly aromatic and sparkling.
It is produced in some of the villages of the provinces of Asti and Alessandria, such as Vesime, Bubbio, Loazzolo, Calmandrana, Acqui Terme and Strevi.

The regulatory body requires a yield of 80 quintals per hectare and minimum alcohol of 11.5%. When fermentation reaches 6% alcohol, it is halted in order to keep the sugar level high enough. Its intense perfumes remind one of strawberries and woodland berries. It is served with biscuits.

Birbet possesses the same characteristics but is classified as a table wine. This is produced in the Roero region of the province of Cuneo. In Piedmontese dialect 'birbet' means a rather naughty child, indicating the lively aspect of the wine.

Brachetto grapes are also used to make a traditionally dry red wine, resembling Dolcetto, which completes its fermentation stage.

SOME MAIN PRODUCERS:
Marenco
Address: Via Vittorio Emanuele 10, 15019 Strevi AL
Telephone: 0144 363133   FAX: 0144 364108
Their organically-produced wines are of excellent quality. They also produce Moscato, Barbera and Dolcetto.

Banfi
Address: Via Vittorio Veneto 22, 15019 Strevi, AL
Telephone: 0144 363485   FAX: 0144 363777
This world-famous winery is run by Giuseppina Viglierchio, an icon of Piedmontese wine. She also produces Asti Spumante, Dolcetto and Gavi.

GRIGNOLINO

This wine's elegance and refined nature have lent, it the title of 'the women's wine'.

There is evidence of its cultivation in the Piedmontese hills from the 18th century. Typical areas of production are the Asti and Casale regions. This wine possesses a lightish purple-red colouring fading at times to a clear pink. It has a medium body and perfumes ranging from fruit and flowers to grass. It possesses moderate acidity and is not overly alcoholic making it an easy-to-drink wine which can be served with various dishes, such as cold meat starters or hot starters to Piedmontese pasta dishes.

The DOC denominations of greatest importance are Grignolino d'Asti and Grignolino del Monferrato Casalese. A DOC of lesser importance is the Piemonte Grignolino. The area of production of Grignolino d'Asti comprises a dozen comunes in the province of Asti, amongst which are Castagnole Lanze, Castagnole Monferrato and Rocchetta Tanaro.

Grignolino del Monferrato Casalese is produced in several comunes in the north of Alessandria province including Serravalle d'Icrea and Vignale Monferrato. For both varieties, the regulatory body permits the addition of 10% Freisa grapes and requires a minimum alcohol level of 11%. No particular period of ageing is required.

Michele Chiarlo
Address: Strada Nizza-Canelli 99, 14042, Calamandrana AT
Telephone: 0141 769030   FAX: 0141 769033
e-mail: chiarlo@tin.it
One of the biggest and most prestigious wineries producing wines of great quality. It also produces Barolo, Barbaresco, Barbera, Moscato, Gavi and Dolcetto.

VERDUNO PELAVERGA

This wine risked extinction in the not-so-remote past. Its rebirth is due to the enthusiasm of local wine producers who have even obtained the DOC denomination as a sign of its excellence. From the few vines left in the 1980s, this wine is now produced in respectable quantities, even allowing it to be exported.

It is an intensely-perfumed wine with a lightish red colouring. Its notes are decidedly spicy with additional flowers and fruit.

It possesses a good structure both in alcohol and tannins and fine body.

It is a wine to be consumed young, 2 or 3 years after production.

It can be served throughout the meal and especially with hot starters and home-made pasta.

AMONG THE FEW PRODUCERS ARE:
Castello Verduno
Address: Via Umberto 1° 9, 12060 Verduno CN
Telephone: 0172 470284   FAX: 0172 470298
This winery is situated in an historical castle and is run by the founder, Cavalier Burlotto's grand daughter Gabriella Burlotto and her husband Franco Bianco. As well as Pelaverga they also produce Barolo and Barbaresco.

Fratelli Alessandria
Address: Via Beato Valfrè 59, 12060, Verduno CN
Telephone + FAX: 0172 470113
This winery was founded at the beginning of the 20the century and is now run by brothers Giovanni and Franco Alessandria. In addition to Pelaverga they also produce Barolo, Barbera and Favorita.

FREISA

This wine possesses similar characteristics to Barbera.

Among the DOC denominations are: Langhe Freisa, Freisa d'Asti and Monferrato Freisa. It is usually produced in the dry, still form but a sweet, fizzy version also exists. The colour is usually ruby-red.

The Langhe Freisa denomination comprises over 90 comunes in the province of Cuneo including the hills around Alba, Barolo and Barbaresco. In the right hands this wine possesses intense floral and fruit perfumes, robust body and good ageing potential owing to its alcohol content of around 12.5%. The regulatory body limits yields to 90 quintals per hectare with a minimum alcohol of 11%. No particular amount of ageing is required.

Freisa d'Asti is produced in the hills around Asti. This is also a wine of quality with ageing of about 12 months for the superior variety. It is also used to produce sweet and sparkling wines. Monferrato Freisa is mostly produced in the province of Alessandria including the Casale area. This wine is only vinified dry and 15% of different grape varieties are allowed in its production.

SOME MAIN PRODUCERS ARE:

Giacomo Conterno
Address: Località Ornati 2, 12065, Monforte d'Alba, CN
Telephone: 0173 78221   FAX: 0173 787190
This winery is now run by the founder's son, Giovanni. Their wines have always been excellent. They also produce one of the finest Barolos in the world (Monfortino) and Barbera.

Poderi Aldo Conterno
Address: Località Bussia 48, 12065 Monforte d'Alba, CN
Telephone: 0173 78150   FAX: 0173 787240
e-mail: www.poderialdoconterno.com
A flower in the button-hole of Piedmontese wine production set among the most precious vineyards in all the Langa. It also produces Barolo, Barbera and Dolcetto.

BLENDS

*hese are wines which are becoming ever more
popular on the modern market.*

They are produced using a blend of 2 or more types of red
grape, usually with a predominance of Nebbiolo, or Barolo or
Barbaresco, plus a quantity of Barbera. Varietals not native to
the area, such as Cabernet Sauvignon, Merlot or Pinot, may
also be used in the blending process.

Producers like to choose imaginative names for these wines,
often with reference to a particular vineyard, a famous historical character or an event which was important for the winery.
It is possible to find wines with names such as Monprà, Arte,
Bricco Rovella, Airone, Bacialè, Seifile and Pin. The wines,
similar in type to Bordeaux, are being accepted on the international market at very high levels.

The blends possess body and structure which are most similar to the wine which forms their base - that is, predominantly
Nebbiolo or Barbera. But they reveal ample and complex flower
and fruit perfumes which are more related to the other varietals
and can be anything from spiced to ethereal. Their freshness
allows for ageing of up to 8 to 12 years and they are usually
treated in barrique.

These wines are ideal for accompanying the main courses of a
Piedmontese meal such as dishes containing wild mushrooms,
red meats, game and fairly matured cheeses. They are divided
into 2 main denominations: Langhe Rosso and Monferrato
Rosso. Sometimes these wines may also be classified as simply
'table wines'.

SOME MAIN PRODUCERS:
Domenico Clerico
Address: Località Manzoni 67, Monforte d'Alba, CN
Telephone: 0173 781171   FAX: 0173 789800
Domenico is one of the Langhe's great eccentric personalities
and also one of its great producers. In addition to his blend
'Arte', he also produces Barolo, Barbera and Dolcetto.

Conterno and Fantino
Address: Via Ginestra 1, 12065 Monforte d'Alba CN

Telephone: 0173 78204   FAX: 0173 787326
e-mail: info@conternofantino.it
Producers of extremely high quality wines, including blends.
Their 'Monprà' opened the way to many others… they also produce Barolo, Barbera, Freisa and Dolcetto.

Parusso
Address: Località Bussia 55, 12065 Monforte d'Alba, CN
Telephone: 0173 78257   FAX: 0173 787276
Marco and Tiziana, brother and sister, founded their winery in
1985 and it is now one of the area's greatest. As well as their
blend, 'Bricco Rovella', they produce Barolo, Barbera and
Dolcetto.

WHITE WINES

Although Piedmont is more famous for its reds, white wines are now asserting themselves in no uncertain way.

Piedmontese white wines, thanks to the traditionally pain-staking Piedmontese approach to production, are becoming ever more popular on the international market and have left the old image of low-cost low-quality wine far behind them. Today, Gavi, Arneis, Favorita and Erbaluce have nothing to fear for their reputations. Moscato d'Asti, too, is now being reconsidered as a wine suitable for aperitifs and not only for consumption with desserts at the end of a meal. All these wines are produced from varietals native to the area and, therefore, owe their quality to the typical characteristics of the Piedmontese climate and terrain. It would be true to say that they are following in the footsteps of the great success of the region's red wines.

Every varietal corresponds to a particular area of the region. Cortese, from which Gavi DOCG is produced, comes from the hills around Alessandria, in the Ovada area near the border with the region of Liguria. Arneis and Favorita are best when grown on the Roero hills around Bra. Erbaluce is from the Canavese area in the province of Turin, whereas Moscato d'Asti is grown on the hills of the area which stretches from Santo Stefano Belbo in the province of Cuneo to Canelli in the province of Asti.

A recent acquisition has been Alta Langa Brut, born from the joining together of several wineries to form a consortium for the production of this wine in the Alta Langa area. We are convinced that this wine has a very rosy future. Ten years of experimentation and investment have gone into its development. Vinification was begun in 2002, after extensive research had demonstrated the ideal nature of the Alta Langa hills in the provinces of Cuneo, Asti and Alessandria for the growing of Chardonnay and Pinot. There is every hope that this area may one day become the 'Champagne' of Italy.

Varietals such as Chardonnay, Sauvignon and Pinot have also found their place in the region and a restricted quantity of excellent wines similar to the French versions are produced with them.

CORTESE

*T*his varietal produces Gavi, the first Piedmontese
white wine to obtain a DOCG denomination.
It is grown in the hills around Ovada in the province of
Alessandria where it borders with the region of Liguria.

Gavi's boom came during the 1980s. These days it can boast a
stable market comprising all those who admire its distinctive
bouquet of white fruit, citrus, hay and almonds. Its colour is a
straw-yellow with greenish highlights when young tending to
golden with age. It is produced within the comunes of Gavi,
Tassarolo and Novi Ligure and the procedure for its DOCG recognition was identical to that for any other wine, including the
grand Barolo.

The regulatory body restricts grape production to 100 quintals
per hectare. Alcohol content must be a minimum of 10.5%,
although this is often exceeded. Gavi is usually best drunk
young, after the first 2 or 3 years. Some producers produce a wine
which, owing to low yields and maturing in oak barrels, can be
aged for longer, up to 7 years. This wine may also be vinified in
a sparkling or spumante version.

The Cortese varietal is also used to produce 2 other types of
white wine: Cortese dell'Alto Monferrato and Piemonte Cortese.
Both these wines possess similar characteristics to Gavi with the
exception that 15% of different grapes may be included in the
vinification process. Production zones are distributed in the provinces of Asti and Alessandria for Cortese dell'Alto Monferrato.
Piemonte Cortese has a wider zone of production which also
includes various comunes in the province of Cuneo.

These wines are ideal for accompanying fish dishes, vegetable
starters and soups.

SOME MAIN PRODUCERS:

Villa Sparina
Frazione Monterotondo 56, 15066 Gavi AL
Telephone: 0143 633835 FAX: 0143 633857
e-mail: sparina@villasparina.it
This winery, founded in the 18th century, is run today by Massimo and Stefano Moccagatta from the lovely villa of the same name surrounded by its vineyards and parkland. They also produce Barbera, Dolcetto d'Acqui, Cortese Metodo Classico.

La Scolca
Frazione Rovereto 15066, Gavi, Al.
Telephone: 0143 682176   FAX: 0143 682197
A classically prestigious winery run by Giorgio Soldati who is also its enologist. It also produces Gavi, Brut and Cortese Brut.

La Giustiniana
Frazione Rovereto 5, 15066 Gavi, AL
Telephone: 0143 682132   FAX: 0143 682085
This winery, run for the last 25 years by the Lombardi family, produces top-quality wines. They also make Cortese and Monferrato Rosso.

ARNEIS

*Arneis has been blessed with a meteoric rise
in fame and prestige during the last 20 years or so,
an event almost without precedent
in the Italian wine world.
The reason for this success is to be found
in those inimitable characteristics such as the intensely
fruity perfumes which render it so pleasing to the palate.
It may be consumed as an aperitif,
with starters or with many other dishes
among the Piedmontese pantheon.
It also filled a gap in the Piedmontese wine market,
bursting with great reds yet, up until Arneis,
rather lacking in superb whites.*

Particular merit for having taken Arneis to the world's best restaurants must be due to Bruno and Marcello Ceretto's version, Blangè.

The most important area of production is the Roero, within a dozen comunes including Canale, Vezza and Castellinaldo. The Langhe Arneis denomination is also of high quality however, extending over a vaster area. Arneis is normally vinified as a dry white wine but spumante and passito versions also exist. It is usually made in stainless steel vats although newer techniques include the use of small wooden barrels. It possesses a straw-yellow colouring which tends to acquire golden highlights with age. Its intense perfumes include green apple, cherry blossom, dried fruits and so on. It is a nicely fresh wine which needs to be consumed a year or two after production. It makes a great aperitif and is perfect to accompany cold Piedmontese starters.

SOME MAIN PRODUCERS:
Fratelli Ceretto
*Località San Cassiano 34, 12051 Alba CN
Telephone: 0173 282582   FAX: 0173 282383
e-mail: ceretto@ceretto.com*

Brothers Bruno and Marcello have done so much for the fame of the area with the distribution of their winery's products around the world. As well as their Blangè Arneis they produce Barolo, Barbaresco, Barbera and Dolcetto.

Bruno Giacosa
Via XX Settembre 52, Neive CN
Telephone: 0173 67027 FAX: 0173 677477
e-mail: brunogiacosa@brunogiacosa.it
Founded at the beginning of the 20th century, this winery is as much an essential part of the Piedmontese and Italian wine world as its owner, Bruno Giacosa. He also produces Barbaresco, Barolo, Barbera and Arneis.

Vietti
Piazza Vittorio Veneto 5, 12060, Castiglione Falletto,CN
Telephone: 0173 62825 FAX: 0173 62941
e-mail: info@vietti.com
One of Piedmont's historical wineries. Great wines and great sensations… they also produce Barolo, Barbera and Nebbiolo.

FAVORITA

*⊂Jhis wine has a short but special history.
Its name probably derives from the fact that it was
King Carlo Alberto's preferred wine, one that he
used to call simply 'my favourite' when ordering his
waiters to serve it. In time, the King's waiters used the
name as shorthand for the wine:
"hurry up and bring the King's favourite...!"*

Since the 1970s, after a period of time during which the grape
risked extinction, the wine has been resurrected thanks to modern
vinification techniques such as the use of stainless steel fermentation vats equipped with thermostats and is becoming ever more
popular as time goes on.

Favorita can be considered Arneis' younger brother, and like
the latter is grown on the Roero hills. Favorita is a light, fruity
wine pleasant on the palate and not overly alcoholic. It is ideal as
an aperitif or when accompanying vegetable starters. It possesses
a straw-yellow colour with green highlights. Its perfumes include white plums, green apples, hawthorn and hazel. It should be
consumed at fairly cool temperatures and within the year following harvest.

FAVORITA: SOME MAIN PRODUCERS
Tenuta Carretta Località Carretta 2, 12040, Piobesi d'Alba, CN
Telephone: 0173 619119 FAX: 0173 619931
e-mail: t.carretta@tenutacarretta.it
During recent years this winery has become a leading light for
wineries of the Roero district. It also produces Barbaresco,
Barbera, Arneis and Dolcetto.

Gianni Gagliardo Borgata Serra dei Turchi 12064, Santa Maria
di La Morra CN Telephone: 0173 50829 FAX: 0173 509230
Gianni Gagliardo was one of Favorita's founding fathers and
also successfully produces other Piedmontese wines such as
Barolo, Dolcetto and Nebbiolo.

Malvirà Case Sparse Canova 144, 12043, Canale, CN.
Telephone: 0173 978145 FAX: 0173 959154
e-mail: malvira@malvira.com. Rightly considered one of the
leading wineries of the entire area. This winery also produces
Roero Superiore, Arneis and Barbera.

ERBALUCE

*This vine is grown in the area around Caluso,
near Ivrea, in the province of Turin. Here,
the hills form a natural amphitheatre of morainal
origin. The wine, Erbaluce di Caluso, or Caluso,
is a gem for any wine buff.*

The most popular version is the passito, which must be aged
for at least 5 years, first in steel and then in wood and bottle
before sale. Its colour is a golden amber varying in intensity
according to the length of ageing. Its perfumes, which are both
intense and delicate, include chestnuts, almonds and dried
fruit.
Erbaluce must possess at least 13.5% alcohol. Caluso Passito
Liquoroso must have a minimum of 17.5%. Both these wines
resist ageing well and are ideal to accompany biscuits or tangy
cheeses. They may also be consumed on their own for sheer pleasure.
Erbaluce is also to be found in a sparkling format (11.5%
alcohol) or the classical version (minimum alcohol 11%).

MOSCATO

*Moscato is probably the most ubiquitously cultivated white grape in Italy.
Without a doubt it produces the most popular Spumantes in the world. Millions of bottles of Asti Spumante and Moscato leave Italy every year to start their journey to a foreign destination.*

An increase in quality in recent years has slightly decreased production but there can be few who have not celebrated a Christmas or some other special occasion with a glass of this sweet sparkling white wine. The Moscato grape is very aromatic and has a high sugar content, giving a wine which is both perfumed and, thanks to the method of vinification used with residual sugars remaining in the wine, also pleasantly sweet. Four main types of wine are produced with this grape: Asti Spumante, Moscato d'Asti, Piemonte Moscato and Loazzolo. The production area extends through the provinces of Cuneo, Asti and Alessandria.

The DOCG denomination was awarded to the first two varieties, Asti Spumante and Moscato d'Asti, in 1993. These wines are similar, differing in alcohol content and volume of sugar fermented (between 5.5 - 6.5% for Moscato and 7 - 9.5% for Spumante). Moscato is thus the sweeter wine of the two. There are also certain differences in bottling. For Moscato a typical wine bottle is used, corked in the usual way. For Spumante a champagne-type bottle is used with the typical champagne cork within a metal cage. Both wines are best served with desserts or biscuits during special occasions. Ladies also seem to particularly appreciate a glass of Moscato as a delicious aperitif!

Piemonte Moscato possesses very similar characteristics to Moscato d'Asti. Loazzolo, product of the homonymous comune, is produced with late-harvested grapes giving very low yields (a maximum of 50 quintals per hectare). It is then aged for at least 2 years including at least 6 months in small wooden casks. This is a true 'cult' wine for wine buffs and is ideal, in addition to accompanying desserts, for consuming together with matured or herb cheeses.

SOME MAIN PRODUCERS:

ASTI SPUMANTE

Fratelli Bera
Via Castellero 12, 12050, Neviglie, CN
Telephone: 0173 630194 FAX: 0173 630394
e-mail: info@bera.it
Walter Bera endorses Moscato with obstinacy, born out by the quality of his excellent wines, which also include reds such as Barbera, Dolcetto and his blend 'Sassisto'.

Contratto
Via G.B. Giuliani 56, 14053, Canelli, AT
Telephone: 0141 823349 FAX: 0141 824650
e-mail: info@contratto.it
An historical winery which produces high quality Asti Spumante and also Barolo and Barbera.

Terrenostre
Località San Martino 8, 12054 Cossano Belbo, CN
Telephone: 0141 88137 FAX: 0141 88509
A co operative winery producing wines which are excellent value for money, including 'Furmentin'.

Il Falchetto
Frazione Ciombi, Via Valtinella 16, 12058, Santo Stefano Belbo, CN
Telephone: 0141 840344 FAX: 0141 843520
Four young brothers are working together to found a winery with a great future. They also make Barbera and Dolcetto.

Sergio Grimaldi
Località San Grato 7, 12058 Santo Stefano Belbo CN
Telephone + FAX: 0141 840341
A small family winery which makes products of high quality.

Scanavino
Località Scorrone 70, 12054 Cossano Belbo CN.
Telephone: 0141 837102
Passion for wine making here produces excellent results in a range of Piedmontese wines.

La Spinetta
Via Annunziatu 17, 14054, Castagnole Lanze AT
Telephone: 0141 877396
Three brothers, a winery, success... Every bunch produces an excellent wine. They also make Barbaresco, Barbera and Moscato.

Passiti

Forteto della Luja
Regione Bricco Casa Rosso 4, 14050 Loazzolo AT
Telephone + FAX: 0141 831596
e-mail: fortetodellaluja@inwind.it
One of Italy's small but historical wineries. To this winery goes the merit of having experimented late-harvested Moscato. They also produce Brachetto and Barbera.

Giuseppe Laiolo
Strada Piancanelli 22, 14050 Loazzolo AT
Telephone: 0144 87287 FAX: 0144 857900
A small family winery well worth a visit. They also produce Barbera.

The Fontanafredda estate. Its buildings are still painted in the colours of the Royal House of Savoy.

ALTA LANGA BRUT

*$\mathcal{T}$This wine possesses the most recently
acquired DOC denomination,
published in the official ministerial
document of 23rd November 2002.*

This date celebrated the appearance of a wine which was the fruit of 10 years of planning, experimentation and investment in the vineyard on the part of various regional bodies and major Piedmontese producers of Spumante wines. 'Alta Langa' is a wine produced exclusively with the traditional 'champenoise' method, with second fermentation in the bottle. Its production zone intends to assume the title of 'Italy's Champagne'.

A total of 149 comunes in the provinces of Cuneo, Alessandria and Asti, among which may be counted the comunes of Alba, Cortemilia, Santo Stefano Belbo, Canelli and Mango, are included in the project. Spumante wines, which may be white, rosè or red, but which must contain a minimum of 90% Chardonnay or Pinot Nero, are produced in these areas. A maximum of 10% of other varieties can be added. Yields must be restricted to 110 quintals per hectare. It is likely that the white version will have predominance, in accordance with market demands.

This wine has a straw-yellow colour with a fine and persistent perlage. Its perfumes are intense and long-lasting and include fresh bread, meadow flowers and green apples. It is an ideal wine for aperitifs or to accompany fish-based meals.

Fontanafredda
Via Alba 15, 12050 Serralunga d'Alba CN
Telephone: 0173 626111   FAX: 0173 613471
e-mail: fontanafredda@fontanafredda.it
This is Vittorio Emanuele II, the King of Italy's, winery, which he founded in 1878. Here, the ideal combination of quality, quantity and value for money are to be found. They also produce Barolo, Moscato and Barbera.

Bersano
Piazza Dante 21, 14049, Nizza Monferrato AT
Telephone: 0141 720211   FAX: 0141 701706
e-mail: wine@bersano.it
A winery with a great past which is preparing itself for a fine future. They also produce Barolo, Barbera, Gavi, Moscato and Arneis.

Cocchi
Via Malta 17, 14100 Asti AT
Telephone: 0141 907083   FAX: 0141 907085
e-mail: cocchi@cocchi.com
Asti's historical winery. They also produce Barolo Chinato and Brachetto.

The champagne method

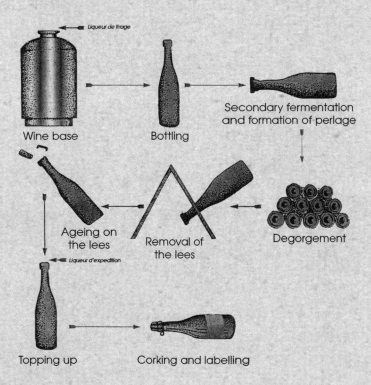

Liqueur de tirage

Wine base

Bottling

Secondary fermentation and formation of perlage

Ageing on the lees

Removal of the lees

Degorgement

Liqueur d'expedition

Topping up

Corking and labelling

PIEDMONT'S REGIONAL WINE CENTRES

Enoteca di Piemonte' is a regional wine consortium, founded by the Region's administration and comprising 10 local wine centres, or 'enoteca', with the aim of stimulating and maintaining interest in the area's marvellous DOC and DOCG wine heritage.

It is the first such network established at a regional and not solely local level in Europe with the intention of promoting wines of quality.

The 10 local Wine Centres are to be found in the comunes of: *Acqui Terme AL, Barolo CN, Barbaresco CN, Canale d'Alba CN, Canelli AT, Gattinara VC, Grinzane Cavour CN, Mango CN, Roppolo BI and Vignale Monferrato AL*. All of these centres are situated in historical castles or other buildings of great historical interest. They receive over 500,000 visitors a year, people who are fascinated by the world of wine. These visitors are attracted to the centres by the accurate information offered there, by the various cultural and informative events organised in them and, naturally enough, by the quality of the products sold there.

These days, most of Piedmont's wine production is covered by the DOC or DOCG denominations. This is a demonstration of Piedmont's position in the world as a bastion of excellence and cultural commitment as represented by its unique wine heritage.

The 'Enoteca del Piemonte' has founded a programme of publicity and promotion, 'Pro Made in Italy', involving all the media to stimulate interest in Italy's values, culture and heritage and in particular the mystery and allure of Piedmont with its 46 DOC and 8 DOCG wines. Each local wine centre also organises various cultural and artistic events every year which add to Piedmont's prestige at world level. Among these are the studies produced by the Roero Wine Centre (CN), which aim to enhance the wines' image and quality and a symposium organised by the same centre on genetically modified species in viticulture.

Other important aspects of the Wine Centre's work include guided tasting sessions, participation at international wine events, wine fairs, enhancement of tourism especially in the areas of wine and food tourism, and stimulation of interest in local agriculture.

The wines presented and sold in the various Wine Centres are exclusively DOC and DOCG labels, selected by a team of experts via blind tasting sessions which are open to the public. A minimum grade of 80/100 is required for a wine to be accepted. Mention must also be made of the more local 'Botteghe Comunali del Vino', wine shops which are situated in various wine municipalities and which promote local wine producers.

ENOTECA DEL PIEMONTE'
Via Nizza 294 - 10126 Turin
Telephone +39 011 6677667 - FAX+39 011 6677646
e-mail: info@enotecadelpiemonte.com

Local Wine Centres:
Enoteca Regionale di Acqui Terme
Piazza Levi, 7, 15011 Acqui Terme, AL - Telephone: 0144 770273

Enoteca Regionale del Barbaresco
Via Torino 8/a, 12050 Barbaresco, CN   Telephone: 0173 635251

Enoteca del Barolo
Piazza Falletti 1, 12060 Barolo, CN - Telephone: 0173 56277

Enoteca del Roero
Via Roma 57, 12043, Canale, CN - Telephone: 0173 978228

Enoteca Regionale di Canelli e dell'Astesana
Corso Libertà 65/a 14053 Canelli, AT - Telephone: 0141 832182

Enoteca Regionale Piemontese 'Cavour'
Via Castello 5, 12060, Grinzane Cavour, CN
Telephone: 0173 262159

Enoteca Regionale di Gattinara e delle Terre del Nebbiolo del Nord Piemonte
Corso Valsesia 112, 13045, Gattinara, VC
Telephone: 0163 834070

Enoteca Regionale Colline del Moscato
Piazza XX Settembre 19, 12056 Mango CN
Telephone: 0141 89291

Enoteca del Monferrato
Palazzo Callori 15049 Vignale Monferrato AL
Telephone: 0142 933243

Enoteca Regionale della Serra
Castello di Roppolo 13883, Roppolo BI - Telephone: 0161 987520

A Piedmontese delegation of the
*'**Donne del Vino**' (Women of Wine) association.*

From the top:
Paola Bera from Villa San Carlo Cortemilia;
Cristina Ascheri from the Ascheri Winery in Bra;
Gabriella Burlotto from the Castello Winery in Verduno;
Gavina Fois from the Pallone restaurant in Bistagno;
Alessandra Buglione from Castello Winery, Verduno;
Ileana Corradini from Villa Ile Winery, Treiso.

"LE DONNE DEL VINO", WOMEN OF WINE

*The Italian national association 'Donne del Vino',
Women of Wine, was formed in 1988 and for
more than 15 years has constituted a group
of producers, restaurant owners, wine centre owners,
sommelier and journalists who all, in their way,
promote wine culture throughout the country.*

Article 3 of the association's statute, entitled 'Aims and
Objectives', reads: 'The Association declares the aim of impro-
ving knowledge of wine using every available means, for example by organising meetings, tasting sessions, debates, round
tables, study holidays and updating courses, with particular
attention to the world of women.'

The Association has about 700 members throughout Italy
including over 200 producers and about 100 restaurant
owners. The Piedmontese delegation is well represented with
around 160 members including producers, restaurant owners,
wine centre owners, sommelier and journalists. This
Association is one of the most active today in the immense
world of wine and food culture and interest.

Secretariat of the Piedmontese delegation:
Viale Umberto I 1, 14049, Nizza Monferrato, AT.
Telephone: 0141 793076 FAX: 0141 793079
Associazione Nazionale Le Donne del Vino
(National Association of Women of Wine):
Via San Vittore al Teatro 3, 20123, Milano

ASSOCIAZIONE NAZIONALE
LE DONNE
DEL VINO
del Piemonte

PRIVATE WINE CENTRES

*In addition to a visit to the Regional Wine Centres,
we advise wine shopping at one or more
of the many private wine centres and shops in
Piedmont, where it is possible to appreciate the varied
products of many different producers.
There is a vast choice available.
The following is merely a small sample:*

- **Carosso**
  Via Vittorio Emanuele 23, 12051, Alba, Telephone: 0173 440600
- **Dei Castelli**
  Corso Torino 14/1 12051, Alba, Telephone: 0173 333511
- **Enolibreria I Piaceri del Gusto**
  Via Vittorio Emanuele 23, Alba, Telephone: 0173 440166
- **Fracchia & Berchialla**
  Via Vernazza 9, 12051, Alba, Telephone: 0173 440508
- **L'Enoteca Artistica**
  Via Dante Alighieri 51, 12074, Cortemilia CN
  Telephone: 0173 81950

ASSESSMENT OF VINTAGES

*A wine is often judged according
to the producer or the name
to be found on the label.*

However, in reality the situation is a little more complicated than this. Wine is made from a fruit which follows a natural cycle of growth and many factors can affect the quality of a vintage. Climactic factors can be of supreme importance, making or breaking a producer's careful work in the vineyard.

Often, knowing who the name refers to on a bottle's label is not enough. It is essential to have information on the meteorological conditions of a given vintage.

The following table has been drawn up to aid you in your selection of recent vintages. Particularly good years ('for your cellar') are indicated. Having said this, I should add that during lesser years, producers are careful to improve the quality of their wines in a perfectly natural way: that is, lowering yields in the vineyard by scrupulous selection of bunches of fruit to use for vinification. This in turn limits the number of bottles produced. During an exceptionally bad year, a producer may decide not to make wine at all. During these years, it is clear that any wine brought out onto the market will be of inferior quality, balanced naturally by subsequent years of excellence.

Legenda:

♥ Average year
♥ ♥ Good year
♥ ♥ ♥ Great year
♥ ♥ ☆ ♥ ♥ Exceptional year, 'for your cellar'

Annata	Barolo	Barbaresco	Brunello	Amarone
1964	♥♥☆♥♥	♥♥☆♥♥	♥♥♥	♥♥☆♥♥
1967	♥♥☆♥♥	♥♥♥	♥♥♥	♥♥☆♥♥
1971	♥♥☆♥♥	♥♥♥	♥♥	♥♥♥
1978	♥♥☆♥	♥♥☆♥♥	♥♥☆♥♥	♥♥
1979	♥♥♥	♥♥♥	♥♥♥	♥♥♥
1982	♥♥☆♥♥	♥♥☆♥♥	♥♥☆♥	♥
1985	♥♥☆♥♥	♥♥☆♥♥	♥♥☆♥	♥♥♥
1988	♥♥☆♥♥	♥♥♥	♥♥☆♥	♥♥☆♥♥
1989	♥♥♥☆♥	♥♥☆	♥	♥
1990	♥♥☆♥♥	♥♥☆♥♥	♥♥☆♥♥	♥♥☆♥♥
1991	♥♥	♥♥	♥♥	♥
1992	♥	♥	♥	♥
1993	♥♥	♥♥	♥♥♥	♥♥♥
1994	♥	♥	♥♥	♥
1995	♥♥♥	♥♥♥	♥♥☆♥♥	♥♥♥
1996	♥♥☆♥	♥♥☆♥♥	♥♥	♥♥
1997	♥♥☆♥	♥♥☆♥♥	♥♥☆♥♥	♥♥☆♥
1998	♥♥☆♥♥	♥♥☆♥	♥♥♥	♥♥
1999	♥♥☆♥♥	♥♥♥	♥♥♥	♥♥
2000	♥♥☆♥♥	♥♥☆♥♥	♥♥♥	♥♥♥
2001	♥♥☆♥♥	♥♥☆♥♥		

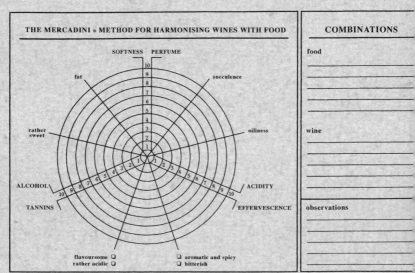

THE MERCADINI ® METHOD FOR HARMONISING WINES WITH FOOD

SOFTNESS   PERFUME
fat
succulence
rather sweet
oiliness
ALCOHOL
ACIDITY
TANNINS
EFFERVESCENCE
flavoursome ☐
rather acidic ☐
☐ aromatic and spicy
☐ bitterish

COMBINATIONS

food

wine

observations

MATCHING FOOD WITH WINE

he Italian Sommelier Association has prepared the following guide to the matching of food with wine.

Generally speaking, the contrast between food and wine in the mouth should be such that the tongue and palate remain dry and clean without either of the two elements prevailing over the other. According to this theory an oil-rich dish such as fillet steak fried with Porcini mushrooms should be accompanied by an alcohol and tannin-rich wine such as Nebbiolo or Barbaresco.

A dish rich in fats such as a risotto with Castelmagno cheese is best accompanied by an acidic wine such as Barbera d'Asti or a lightly sparkling one such as a Brut or a dry but sparkling Freisa. Spicy or very flavoursome dishes such as curried meats ought to be accompanied by soft perfumed wines.

The wine's body should always be matched to the dish in question. It is important that the body of the wine should not override the taste of the food or, on the contrary, not be structured enough for it. Obviously, the permutations are endless both in the wine and food categories. It is possible to accompany oil-rich dishes with other oily food, for instance. Sometimes the correct combination of food and wine is not easy to find and often a certain amount of experience is required to choose the wine with the right characteristics for the occasion.

One thing is certain and that is that desserts must be accompanied by sweet wines and not dry Spumantes. A slice of Christmas Panettone or hazelnut cake requires a glass of good Moscato, Asti Spumante or Brachetto to wash it down!

Sommelier associations both at national and regional level organise courses of tasting and wine appreciation and there is no better way to learn about this fascinating world. The following is a aide-memoir to the correct combination of wine with food:

succulent / oil-rich = alcohol / tannin
fatty / tendency to sweetness = acidity / effervescence
spicy / bitterish or flavoursome /
tendency to acidic = soft / perfumed.

HÔTEL CENTRAL & CONTINENTAL

· · · TORINO

G. COLOMBINI, Propr.

WILD & Ci – MILANO21913

An attractive Art Nouveau menu from the early 20ᵗʰ century

MATCHING THE WINE TO THE COURSE.
SERVING TEMPERATURES:

SPUMANTES $8° - 9°c$
as an aperitive or throughout the meal
(Cortese and Arneis Spumante)

DRY WHITE OR ROSÈ WINES $10° - 11°c$
light starters or fish
(Arneis, Favorita or Chardonnay)

SWEET WHITE OR ROSÈ WINES $12° - 13°c$
desserts
(Moscato d'Asti, Asti Spumante)

LIGHTLY TANNIC YOUNG RED WINES $14° - 15°c$
hot starlers, white meats
(Dolcetto, Grignolino, Barbera)

STRUCTURED RED WINES $16° - 17°c$
red meats, matured cheeses
(Nebbiolo, matured Barbera)

GRAND MATURED RED WINES $18° - 19°c$
game, braised meats
(Barbaresco, Barolo)

PASSITO OR FORTIFIED WINES $8° - 18°c$
tangy matured cheeses, desserts
(Loazzolo, Moscato or Arneis Passito)

Traditional distillation of grappa.
Above: a bottle of grappa labelled personally by the Author.

GRAPPA

*G*rappa is made from distilled pomace, that is the pressed skins left over after a wine has been racked. Until a few years ago its reputation was of a rather poor-quality spirit mostly consumed in bars but all this has changed dramatically over recent years.

Now, with the growth of wine culture in general, grappa has made a come-back, there are grappa tastings and a host of grappa characteristics to discover. Grappa is now classified according to the wine base used (for example Barolo, Moscato or Barbera) or according to vineyard.

In the past, wine producers would hand over their pomace to the distillers of grappa for a few pence but now they themselves pay the distiller to produce a grappa bearing their own name to sell to their own clients. Obviously, this is now a quality product and prices have risen accordingly.

Distillation of grappa is subject to extremely stringent state regulations and few firms possess this licence. Historical distilleries such as Bocchino and Beccaris are to be found in the Canelli area of the province of Asti but there are others in Piedmont and some do sell direct to the public (see below):

Berta
Address: Via Roma, 4 - 14012 Fontanile (AT)
Telephone: 0141 721358

Castelli Giuseppe
Address: Corso Luigi Einaudi, 21 - 12074 Cortemilia (CN)
Telephone: 0173 81093

Francoli F.lli
Address: Via Romagnano, 20 - 28074 Ghemme (NO)
Telephone: 0163 844711

Santa Teresa dei f.lli Marolo
Address: Corso Canale, 105/1 - 12051 Alba (CN)
Telephone: 0173 33144

Sibona
Address: Via Roma, 10 - 12040 Piobesi d'Alba (CN)
Telephone: 0173 610504

Valverde
Address: Str. Olla, 23 - 12074 Cortemilia (CN)
Telephone: 0173 81110

A herd of sheep grazing in the Alta Langa area

MEAT
SALAMI AND
CHEESE

BEEF
SALAMI
CHEESE:
BRA
RASCHERA
CASTELMAGNO
TOMA PIEDMONTESE
ROBIOLE
GORGONZOLA
GRANA PADANO

BEEF

All of the Piedmont region but especially the province of Cuneo and most of all, the Alba and Asti areas, are renowned for the production of top-quality beef.

The breed of choice for both the production of milk and meat is the 'Piedmontese', a native to the area which has developed over the past 30 000 years and has strongly influenced the agriculture of this region. Typical of this breed is the white coat in the adult cow, whereas the calf is wheat-coloured and the bull has darker markings on the legs. The bull is of extremely muscular build, especially at the thigh and the meat is typically tender, tasty and very low in cholesterol (it is said, lower even than sole or chicken). In fact, Piedmontese beef has received recognition at international level owing to its superb nutritional qualities.

These cattle are suitable for keeping both in sheds or outdoors, or a combination of both. For this reason, they are also suitable for mountain pasturing for the production of top-quality cheeses such as Raschera, Bra and Castelmagno.

The breed has obtained success in other areas of the world, for example Mexico, Canada, Brazil, Argentina and the USA. Recently, an agreement was signed between Piedmontese agricultural organisations and the Research Institute of Animal Husbandry to introduce Piedmontese cattle in Mongolia.

In Piedmont itself, the organisation of Consortiums of both cattle farmers and butchers has been encouraged by the Regional Council for Agriculture the better to ensure quality at all levels.

FOR INFORMATION:
Asprocarne Piemontese, Via Silvio Pellico, 10 - 10022 Carmagnola (TO)
Telephone: 011 9715308

Bucolic tranquillity: as well as the calf there are 2 cats waiting for their share of the milk!

SALAMI

*One of the most fascinating aspects
of the Piedmontese world of food and drink are
the stories associated with the 'massacrin',
the dialect word for the itinerant pig-butcher.*

"At the beginning of November, just after the All-Saints holiday, when the very last bunches of Nebbiolo were safe in the cellars, the 'massacrin' would sharpen his knives and begin his journey up to the hill farms..." A typical story might have begun like this, as a grandmother from times past rocked her grandchild in front of the glowing embers in the hearth.

It was at the beginning of the autumn that farming families celebrated the grape harvest and the killing of their pig. The best cuts of pork would be sold to 'gentlemen' or to the village butchers, while the blood, offal and lesser cuts would be utilised to prepare a big party. The women of the farm used pig blood to make blood pudding and lasagna whereas a dish known as 'Finanziera', ('frock coat') was concocted with the lungs, heart and liver of the animal. 'Frizze', a kind of meatball, were also made with offal. In the evening, the family met together to eat and celebrate with wine and song.

The 'massacrin', aided by the men of the house, would prepare salamis for the household, which could be kept throughout the following year or sold. In the absence of refrigerators or electricity, the salting and drying of meat was essential for its preservation. This said, salami, sausages, lard, bacon and coppa were among the most delicious results of the pig-killing.

These days, the 'massacrin' has almost completely disappeared from the countryside pantheon for reasons of hygiene but Piedmontese butchers and salami-makers continue to benefit from this age-old tradition. Sometimes however, the 'massacrin' will resurface when country families produce salamis for home consumption. Techniques haven't changed that much over the years with the exception of hygiene: these days a sterile environment is required. Modern salami butchers use their grandparents recipes, using a touch of their own imagination to create new taste sensations.

The following is a sample of traditional Piedmontese salamis:

Fresh-meat salamis are made with raw pork, flavoured with salt, pepper and spices and slowly seasoned in underground cellars. Cooked salamis contain garlic and strips of lard, flavours and spices. They are marinated in red wine in small oak barrels and then steamed. Lard is prepared from the pig's underbelly and is salted and seasoned with the herbs and spices which give it its delicate flavour. 'Cacciatorini' (literally 'little hunters') are small uncooked salamis once consumed by hunters as they prowled the countryside. A world-famous type of sausage is made in Bra and other pork products include cooked and uncooked hams and bacon.

Among the newer generations of salami there are those with innovative flavourings such as Barolo, hazelnuts, garlic and truffle. A special mention should be made of the fillet salami, in ever greater request. This contains a fillet of pork at its heart which is salted and seasoned together with the rest of the salami.

Other specialities of the Piedmontese world of salamis include those made with meats other than pork, for instance donkey meat, wild boar, deer (difficult to find but well worth it) and beef salami.

CHEESE

Cheese has always been an important part of the everyday Piedmontese diet. Easy to keep, cheese was a nutritious element of the meals of even the poorest inhabitants of the mountain valleys.

Nearly every mountain or hill-farming family possessed milk-producing animals such as cows, sheep or goats and could therefore also produce their own cheese which could then be seasoned and consumed over long periods of time. These days, after a period of time during which the cheese industry seemed to be risking extinction, there is renewed interest in the sector and gourmets have rediscovered Piedmontese cheeses, encouraging this age-old culinary art and halting the exodus of cattle farmers from the mountain valleys.

In 1996, the European Union awarded 8 Piedmontese cheeses a DOP ('Denominazione d'Origine Protetta' or protected zone of origin) denomination. These are Castelmagno, Bra, Raschera, Toma Piemontese, Robiole or Tume (from Murazzano and Roccaverano), Gorgonzola and Grana Padano. These are but a few of the many cheeses produced in Piedmont. Everywhere you go there will be a farmer who produces his own cheese according to age-old traditions, each cheese unique in its way. Among the DOP cheeses each has its own Consortium to guarantee quality.

Piedmont produces about 800,000,000 litres of milk and of these, 43% comes from the province of Cuneo and of this 70% is destined for the production of cheese.

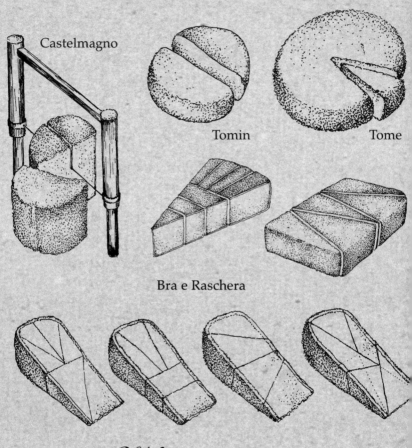

Castelmagno

Tomin

Tome

Bra e Raschera

*Ways of cutting different cheeses,
a useful tip for experts and amateurs alike*

Thus, in the province of Cuneo alone, every year over 30,000,000 kilos of cheese are made.

Piedmontese restaurants have played a key role in the rediscovery of the region's cheeses, promoting local varieties including rarities. Some cooks offer a wide variety of local cheeses on their menus, often presenting them as a main dish or as a tasty alternative to the meat course. The cheese industry has also worked hard to encourage the consumer to try its wide range of fresh and seasoned cheeses. On the following pages the reader will find a guide to the best-known Piedmontese cheeses plus a list of seasoners and outlets.

FOR INFORMATION:
Camera di Commercio di Cuneo, Via Emanuele Filiberto, 3 - 12100 Cuneo
Telephone: 0171 318711 - fax 0171 696581
e-mail: info@cn.camcom.it

BRA

This cheese takes its name from the
homonymous town in the province of Cuneo,
once the main centre of production.

Once, cheeses with diverse characteristics were grouped together under the umbrella of 'Formaggio di Bra' or 'Bra Cheeses'. Today, the Bra classification contains 2 categories, Bra Tenero, or tender, and Bra Duro, or hard. Production has spread to the entire province of Cuneo and the mountain version can bear the label 'Alpeggio' indicating its Alpine origin.

Both varieties are cylindrical in form with a diameter of between 30 to 40 cm and from 7 to 9 cm in height. Liquid rennet may be added and these cheeses contain sparsely-distributed small holes. Bra Tenero has a more elastic consistency and is ivory-white in colour. It has a pleasant, delicate perfume and sweetish flavour. It is salted in brine for 36 hours and matured for a minimum of 45 days.

Bra Duro is ochre-yellow in colour and has an intense, tangy flavour with a hint of almonds. It may contain some sheep's or goat's milk. It undergoes dry salting for 3 days per side and is matured for a minimum of 6 months.

This cheese is best accompanied by a young, medium-bodied wine such as Dolcetto or Barbera. It is suitable for the preparation of hot stuffed starters or fondues.

RASCHERA

*This cheese has been made since the 1400's
in 9 comunes of the Val Casotto and Mondovì areas
in the province of Cuneo.*

Its name derives from the antique word 'Ruscaria', the name of its zone of origin. It is produced using cow's milk from 2 different milkings. The milk is coagulated at 27°c – 30°c using liquid rennet in wooden containers which can be round or square. It has a thin crust which is pinkish-grey in colour with yellow highlights. The cheese has an elastic consistency and is ivory-white in colour with small irregular holes. This cheese undergoes dry salting after it has been pressed in stone presses. It must be matured for at least 30 days.

It possesses a fine and delicate flavour in the fresh versions tending to tangy as maturation progresses. If the cheeses has been made over 900 metres above sea level it may bear the label 'Alpeggio'. As with Bra, this cheese may be eaten by itself accompanied by a young red wine such as Dolcetto or Barbera. A grander red may be chosen to accompany the more matured versions. In the kitchen it is used to prepare fondues and hot starters.

CASTELMAGNO

This cheese takes its name from the homonymous town in the Grana valley a few kilometres from Cuneo. The reulatory body authorises it to be made exclusively with cow's milk produced in the Alpine meadows of Castelmagno, Pradleves and Monterosso Grana.

Its production is documented as far back as the year 1200 and it was appreciated by Charlemain and the popes of Avignon.

It is cylindrical in shape with a thin, yellowish-red crust which is smooth when fresh. As the cheese matures the crust becomes more wrinkly and darker in colour. The cheese is semi-hard and chalky in consistency. It is ivory-yellow in colour tending to gold with green veins appearing as maturing progresses. When young, its flavour is delicate and fairly salty becoming tasty and tangy with age.

Raw milk from 2 different milkings is used. The cows are pastured in meadows which are particularly rich in aromatic herbs. Coagulation occurs over an hour with 2 interruptions of curdling a few days apart from one another. After curdling the cheese is shaped in the classical cylindrical forms and then pressed. Maturation can last from 2 to 5 months.

Castelmagno is excellent eaten on its own accompanied by full-bodied, perfumed wines such as Nebbiolo or Barbera. It is also frequently used to prepare dishes such as risotto or gnocchi (potato dumplings) in Castelmagno sauce.

GORGONZOLA

*T*his is one of the best-known Italian
cheeses world-wide. It comes from the provinces of
Novara (about 50% of total production),
Vercelli, Verbania-Cusio-Ossola, Cuneo and
Casale in Piedmont. It is also produced in Lombardy.

Historically, it is mentioned in the will of the Milan archbishop
Ansperto da Biassono in the year 800.

Gorgonzola is made with whole cow's milk from a single milking
which is coagulated at 28°c- 30°c using calf's rennet. Penicillin
spores and lactobacilli are added to give it the classic blue-green
veins which appear during seasoning. It is a white, soft, full-fat
cheese containing large quantities of vitamins and minerals.

It is cylindrical in shape, each cylinder weighing from 6 to 13 kg.
Maturation usually takes place in refrigerators at a temperature
between 2°c to 7°c. The flavour is sweet with a pleasant tang of
mould. Gorgonzola Naturale, the natural version, is aged for
months in grottoes. This cheese is harder and less creamy than the
usual variety and more decidedly tangy.

Gorgonzola is a versatile cheese, ideal for spreading on crusty
bread or on sticks of celery. It can also be used to prepare risottos
and gnocchi or to make hot sauces. It is best accompanied by matured white 'passito' wines or grand reds such as Barolo or
Barbaresco.

GRANA PADANO

This cheese's main production area is to be found on the Padana plain in Lombardy but it is also officially made in Piedmont, especially within the province of Cuneo.

There are different theories on the origins of its name. The official version states that this derives from the word 'granulosa' or grainy, indicating the cheese's texture. Another theory declares that it comes originally from the Grana valley in the province of Cuneo, home also to Castelmagno which is similar in texture and appearance. Historical documents attest to a cheese with characteristics very similar to Grana Padano which was consumed by Cistercian monks of Chiaravalle in the year 1000.

This is a cheese created for long-term preservation. It is made from half-cream cow's milk and possesses a hard, grainy texture. It is matured slowly becoming straw-yellow in colour. The cylinders weigh from between 24 to 40 kg. The crust is hard, oiled and golden-yellow in colour. Salting lasts from 17 to 28 days and ageing is for a minimum of 8 months in a temperature-controlled environment.

This cheese is used, grated, to season all sorts of pasta dishes. It is also ideal eaten on its own accompanied by one of the grand red wines.

ROBIOLE

*In Piedmontese dialect these cheeses are known as 'Tume'. The officially recognised varieties, that is, those with a DOP denomination, are the Robiola from Murazzano and that from Roccaverano, which take their names from their homonymous villages.
Other types of Robiola are made under other names all over Piedmont.*

Robiola **Murazzano** is a full-fat, soft cheese made either with sheep's milk or with a mixture of cow's, sheep's and goat's milk in varying quantities. Production is limited to the Alta Langa area and a few outlying villages. This cheese is cylindrical in shape with a diameter of between 10   15cm and a height of about 4 cm. There is no crust and the cheese is white in colour, tending to yellow when matured, with a fairly soft consistency. It possesses a delicate flavour when fresh becoming tastier, even tangy when aged. It is sometimes seasoned using natural elements such as fig leaves, ash and aromatic herbs. These additions must be indicated on the label.

The Robiola **Roccaverano** is similar to that of Murazzano in production techniques and flavour. Production is limited to Roccaverano and a few other villages in the Asti area.

Robiola is a traditional feature of Piedmontese cuisine. These days it is eaten together with other typical products of the area, such as hazelnuts, or is used as an ingredient of the stuffing of 'Ravioli al Plin'. Piedmontese elders used to consume Robiola cheeses at tea-time with a glass of young, perfumed Dolcetto.

Some cheese-makers have begun to publicise single Robiola Roccaverano 'crus' following on from the use of the names of single vineyards in wine production. This distinguishes small-time producers and enhances each product's unique properties.

TOMA PIEMONTESE

This cheese is made with cow's milk in the provinces of Turin, Cuneo, Biella, Novara, Verbania and Vercelli plus some areas of the provinces of Asti and Alessandria.

It is a delicately-flavoured cheese. Cylindrical in shape, it comes in 2 different sizes, the large version which weighs from 6 to 8 kg with a diameter of 24 – 35 cm and the small version weighing from 1.8 to 5.9 kg and a diameter of between 15 to 25 cm. There are 2 main varieties, Toma Piemontese and Half-fat Toma Piemontese. The first has a smooth, elastic crust yellow when fresh and becoming brownish with ageing. This cheese is white or pale yellow in colour punctured with tiny holes. Its perfumes bring butter and cream to mind and its flavour is slightly acidic. The cheese is salted in brine o dry salting can be used for a period from 15 to 60 days according to size.

The second variety has a less elastic crust of a more intense yellow colour tending to red. It possesses more intense perfumes and a more aromatic flavour. It is made with milk from at least 2 milkings. Calf rennet is used to coagulate the milk at a temperature of around 32 to 35°c. Maturing is for a period of from 15 to 60 days according to the size. In fact this cheese is more adapted to maturing.

Toma Piemontese is ideal to eat by itself or with salads and oven-cooked vegetables. It is best accompanied by a young, perfumed wine.

OTHER CHEESES

Seirass is a type of ricotta matured in hay

Testun, produced in the valleys surrounding Mondovì, is made with cow's and sheep's milk, is square in shape and possesses an intense, rather tangy flavour.

Sora Sola is also made in the Mondovì valleys and in the Valcasotto area. Both cow's and sheep's milk are used. It is usually round in shape, possessing a sweetish flavour when fresh tending to tangy with maturing.

Bettelmatt comes from the Ossolane valleys and is a very rare cheese. It is made at over 2000 m up in the mountains from cow's milk. It has a compact consistency and a favour reminiscent of the mountain herbs of that area.

Blu di Capra is a very tasty blue goat's cheese similar to Gorgonzola Naturale.

Escarun is made with sheep's milk or a mixture of cow's and sheep's milk and is similar to Castelmagno.

WHERE TO BUY CHEESES

Today there are many outlets for cheese
in Piedmont, including specialist shops.
Every town, large or small, has supermarkets
and smaller shops where quality local cheeses
can be bought. Weekly markets are also a
good source of cheeses.

In the countryside, many cheese producers also sell their
wares to the public. A visit to a farm where cheese is made
makes an interesting day out and you might be lucky enough to
make the discovery of some fascinating rarity of the
Piedmontese cheese world!

The following is a list of cheese producers:
- **Arbiora**
  Via Consortile, 18 - Bubbio (AT) - Telephone: 0144 852010

- **Brandone Gianpiero**
  Via Cortemilia, 17 - Perletto (CN) - Telephone: 0173 832159

- **Caseificio Alta Langa**
  Via Provinciale, 17 - Bosia (CN) - Telephone: 0173 854174

- **Cora Stagionatura**
  Via Circonvallazione, 6 - 12077 Monesiglio (CN)
  Telephone: 0174 92418

- **Colombo Franco Az. Agricola**
  Via Gorretta, 2 - Torre Bormida (CN) - Telephone: 0173 88089

- **CO.ZOO A.L.**
  Bg Cornati, 41 - Murazzano (CN) - Telephone: 0173 791184

- **Occelli Agrinatura**
  Reg. Scarrone, 2 - Farigliano (CN) - Telephone: 0173 746411

Piedmontese Cuisine

Recipes

The 'Via del Sale' or 'Salt Road' ran from
Liguria to Piedmont. Cortemilia was a reference point
for the transport of olive oil.

*P*iedmont is justly famous not only for its
wines but also for its cuisine.
Piedmontese cuisine has a long history and
deep roots in the region. Its essence is to be found in
fresh, top- quality ingredients and, at its core,
are the traditional recipes of countless past cooks.
The abundant variety of succulent dishes
varies from valley to valley and is the product
of centuries of creativity.

The rulers of the House of Savoy at the beginning of the 18th
century were among the first to appreciate the importance of a
fine and elaborate cuisine. In 1863, Giovanni Valardi, cook and
pastry-cook of the Turin Royal Family, wrote one of the first
books where the recipes and menus employed during Royal occasions were described. With an almost obsessive eye for detail,
decoration and every possible permutation of wine with food to
offer to guests, Valardi presents us with a portrait of the Royal
cuisine of the era, at both every day and banquet levels.

The excellence of Piedmontese food, as with its wines, is to be
found in the quality of the natural environment and the toil and
dedication of man which combine to produce ingredients of first-
class quality. Every corner of Piedmont boasts its own particular
speciality dish or product, appreciated by an ever -growing number of gourmets. In passing, we might mention the white truffle
of Alba, Nizza's cardoons, Cuneo's marron chestnuts, peppers
from Carmagnola, rice from Vercelli, Cortemilia's hazelnuts and
wild mushrooms from Ceva. It is with these excellent ingredients
that Piedmontese cooks have long prepared their exquisite dishes.

Most of the recipes that we find today, both in Piedmont's
restaurants and in private homes (there is nothing more enjoyable for a Piedmontese than a traditional family gathering and
banquet), are based on those handed down from mother to daughter over many generations. Starters such as 'carne cruda
all'albese' (raw beef prepared with olive oil and lemon juice and
flavoured with garlic), 'vitello tonnato' (cold sliced veal with
tuna mayonnaise), 'insalata russa' (vegetable salad in mayonnaise), or 'peperoni in bagna cauda' (peppers in garlic and anchovy
sauce), all possess a centuries-long history yet, with the occasio-

nal variant, are still found on the menus of today's best restaurants.

Among first courses, we could mention Piedmont's famous 'tajarin' egg noodles or 'ravioli ripieni' made originally to use up any spare pieces of meat after home butchering. Rice dishes, the various 'risottos', are a Piedmontese staple. Meat also features prominently, and whether game or 'Fassone' beef - that is beef derived from the prestigious Piedmontese breed of cattle - is prepared in many tasty ways. Cheeses, of which there are an infinite variety, are also an important part of the cuisine. Entirely home-made until only a few decades ago, both fresh and matured cheeses may be enjoyed.

The realm of desserts has long belonged to both imaginative grandmothers and professional pastry cooks. 'Bunet', an egg pudding made with cocoa and 'amaretti' biscuits is one. Others which need mentioning are 'panna cotta', hazelnut cake, apple or chestnut tarts and 'baci di dama', (small chocolate biscuits), to name but a few.

Local variations on these themes mean that originality is never lost when touring Piedmont's restaurants. The cuisine has been further enriched, since the beginning of the 20th century, by the presence of the 'Via del Sale', the salt roads which led from the Riviera into Piedmont. Goods such as olive oil, asparagus, artichokes and salted fish were transported along these roads from Liguria to Alba, and vice versa, cheeses, potatoes and hazelnuts made their way from Piedmont into the sea-board region. It is for this reason that ingredients such as anchovies became introduced into Piedmontese cuisine, for instance in the dish 'bagna cauda', a local speciality which is a sauce concocted from this fish, garlic and olive oil. On the other hand, 'vitello tonnato', is a hybrid, combining Ligurian olive oil and tuna with Piedmontese veal.

On the following pages the reader will find a selection of typical tasty Piedmontese recipes using traditional ingredients.

Raw beef in the Alba style with white truffle

Ingredients:

600g of raw Fassone fillet steak cut in
very thin slices
30g white Alba truffles
Juice of $^1/_2$ lemon
1 clove of garlic
Salt and pepper to taste
100 ml olive oil
Parmesan to garnish

Method:
Prepare a garnish with the olive oil, lemon juice and garlic and leave for at least 2 hours. Arrange the slices of
meat on a plate and pour over garnish at the moment of
serving. Decorate with fine scales of Parmesan and
grate over truffle to taste.

Celery salad with tuma cheese and hazelnuts

Ingredients:

$^1/_2$ *lemon*
$^1/_2$ *tuma cheese*
Salt and pepper to taste
100g Piedmontese hazelnuts, roughly ground
White celery
3 tablespoons extra virgin olive oil

Method
Cut the celery and tuma cheese into small cubes and mix together with the ground hazels, oil and lemon juice. Serve cooled.

Chicken and chestnut gelatine

Ingredients:

400g chicken breast
200g boiled chestnuts
Fresh rosemary
2 bay leaves
300ml water
1 cube gelatine
100 ml whipped cream
20g black truffle
A few drops of balsamic vinegar or
Passito wine to flavour the gelatine

Method
Prepare the gelatine using the cube and water. Leave to
cool. Put 1/4 of the gelatine in the bottom of a mould and
place in the fridge. Cook the chicken breast in the water
with the rosemary and bay leaves for 15 minutes and cut
into small cubes. Finely slice the chestnuts and truffle
and mix with the chicken. Whip the cream separately
and add to the mixture with the salt and pepper and the
rest of the gelatine. Mix well and add to the mould.
Leave to set in the fridge for a couple of hours then turn
onto a serving plate.

Pepper and cardoon pastries with bagna cauda

Ingredients:

1 portion ready-to-use puff pastry
1 red or yellow pepper
1 cardoon
3 cloves of garlic
6 salted anchovy fillets
$^1/_2$ litre extra virgin olive oil

Method

Roll out the pastry and cut 6 rounds 10 cm in diameter. Brush the tops with egg yolk and cook for 10 minutes in the oven preheated to 220°c. Prepare the bagna cauda: finely chop the garlic and place in a small saucepan with the anchovy fillets. Cover with the olive oil and cook over a low heat until the anchovies have dissolved. Cut the peppers and cardoon into small cubes and add to the bagna cauda. When the pastries are ready, remove them from the oven and cut them open, keeping the tops. Scoop out a hole in the middle and fill with the bagna cauda mixture. Cover with the pastry tops and serve hot.

Bra fondue with white truffle

Ingredients:

> 100g Fontina cheese cut into small cubes
> 1 egg yolk
> 1 tablespoon flour
> Milk to cover
> White Alba truffle to flavour
> (about 10g per portion)

Method
Put the egg yolk and the Fontina into a saucepan and cover with the milk. Add the flour. Cook over a low heat stirring in the same direction. Serve when the cheese has melted and the mixture is dense and creamy. Grate over the truffle.

Carmagnola yellow pepper soup

Ingredients:

100g yellow peppers
$^{1}/_{2}$ chicken broth
$^{1}/_{2}$ onion
1 glass extra virgin olive oil
30g butter
30g plain flour
Fresh rosemary to flavour

Method

Finely chop the onion and fry in the olive oil. Add the yellow peppers, finely chopped and stir for a few minutes over a low heat. Add the butter and flour. When the mixture has blended well add the broth and bring to the boil. Leave to cook for 5 minutes and blend in a blender. Serve in soup plates. Decorate with rosemary leaves and a drizzle of oil.

Piedmontese potato dumplings with hazelnuts

Ingredients:

1 kg potatoes
250g plain flour
200g hazelnuts
2 eggs
10g salt

Method
Boil the potatoes in their skins for 30 minutes, peel and mash them then leave them to cool. Add the flour, hazelnuts, eggs and salt and mix well. Roll out the mixture into sausage shapes then cut it into pieces the size of walnuts. Cook the gnocchi in salted boiling water. Drain them as soon as they start to bob to the surface of the water and garnish with the butter, some olive oil, 2 leaves of sage and a handful of grated Parmesan.

Piedmontese egg noodles with boletus mushrooms

Ingredients for the pasta:

¹/₂ *kg plain flour*
6 egg yolks
3 egg whites

For the sauce (serves 4): 300g fresh boletus mushrooms
1 glass of dry white wine
100 ml extra virgin olive oil
1 clove of garlic
Salt and pepper to taste

Method
Prepare the pasta: make a little volcano with the sifted flour and break the whole eggs plus the yolks into the top of it. Mix well for about 10 minutes. Using a rolling pin roll out the pasta very thinly on a wooden board. With a sharp knife cut the pasta into fairly thick strands, then roll them and cut into much finer strands. Cook in boiling water for a few minutes only.
Prepare the sauce: wash and finely cut the mushrooms. Heat the garlic in the olive oil and add the mushrooms, some chopped parsley and the salt and pepper. Cook thoroughly and add the wine. When the wine has evaporated continue cooking over a low heat for a further 10 minutes, adding a little broth if necessary. When ready, remove the garlic and add the sauce to the cooked pasta, mixing well.

Piedmontese ravioli

Ingredients for the pasta:

> $^1/_2$ kg plain flour
> 6 eggs
> 1 glass warm water

Method
Mix all the ingredients together for at least 10 minutes and roll out very thinly on a wooden board.

For the filling:
> Nettle leaves
> $^1/_2$ onion
> Fresh rosemary
> 1 clove of garlic
> A walnut-sized piece of butter
> Olive oil
> Boiled chopped vegetables
> Small pieces of beef or pork
> 1 egg
> Pepper and nutmeg
> Grated Parmesan

Method
Fry the onion with the garlic and the herbs then remove the garlic. Add the meat, cut into small cubes and when this is cooked add the white wine. When the wine has evaporated add a little water, add salt and pepper to taste and cook half-covered with the lid. Put the cooked meat and vegetables through a mincer and then add both together in a frying pan with the butter. Add the nutmeg and leave to cool then add the egg to make a paste.

How to make the ravioli:
Place a small amount of filling, about the size of a hazel-nut, on the pasta. Then close it with a pinch (the 'plin')
and cut around it with the pasta cutter.

Rice with gorgonzola

Ingredients:

500g rice
50g onion
Extra virgin olive oil
A small piece of butter
50g cream
50g grated Parmesan
200g Gorgonzola
1 glass white wine
Meat broth

Method
Chop the onion finely and fry in the olive oil. Add the rice and cook until golden. Add the wine and let it eva-porate. Add the broth to cover the rice and cook for 15 minutes, if necessary adding further broth. When cooked, add the cream, butter and Gorgonzola. Leave to blend for 2 minutes and serve with a sprinkling of Parmesan.

Nettle or spinach pasta with chestnuts

Ingredients:

300g plain flour
50g boiled nettles or spinach
4 eggs
200g boiled chestnuts
50 ml extra virgin olive oil
A small piece of butter
A pinch of chili pepper

Method
Knead the flour with the eggs and the finely chopped boiled nettles for at least 10 minutes. Cut the pasta into thin strips with a knife. Break up the boiled chestnuts into small pieces in a frying pan and add the oil, butter and chili.
Cook the pasta in plenty of boiling water and mix thoroughly with the chestnut mixture.

Fassone beef fillet with Langa honey

Ingredients:

6 Fassone beef fillets of about 150g each
Plain flour
100 ml Arneis
30 g butter
50 g Acacia honey
30 g orange peel
$^1/_2$ glass extra virgin olive oil
Chopped parsley
Salt and pepper

Method

Flour the steaks lightly and cook them in the olive oil in a frying pan. Drain off the oil, add the wine and cook first over a high flame. Then turn down the heat and cook for a further 2 minutes per side adding the butter, salt and pepper. Before serving drizzle the honey over the steaks and add the parsley and chopped orange peel.

Pieces of chicken
with cardoons

Ingredients:

600 g chicken breast
100 ml Arneis
50 g fresh cream
Salt and pepper
Parsley
200 g cardoons
1 clove of garlic

Method
Cut the chicken into cubes, flour them and fry them in
the hot olive oil. Drain off the oil and add the Arneis,
turning up the heat. Add the cooked cardoons, the cream
and salt and pepper to form a creamy mixture.

To prepare the cardoons:
wash the cardoons in running water and cut them into
thin strips. Fry the garlic in olive oil and add the cardoons. Cook over a low heat adding white wine. When
they are cooked, add parsley and pepper.

Coffee cream dessert

Ingredients:

100 g whipped cream
1 white of egg, whipped
1 yolk beaten with 50 g sugar
20 g soluble coffee powder

Method
Mix the cream, whipped egg white, the yolk beaten with
the sugar and the coffee powder together and put into the
freezer until ready to serve.

1 PACKET = 11 GRAMS = .40 oz

Cortemilia
hazelnut cake

Ingredients:

4 eggs
1 tablespoon flour
150 g sugar
1/2 packet baking powder
200 g toasted and ground hazelnuts

Method
Separate the yolks from the whites and whip the whites until they are stiff. Beat the sugar with the yolks until creamy then add the toasted hazels, flour and baking powder. Add the whipped whites and pour into a cake tin. Cook in the oven at 180°c for about 30 minutes.

Grandmother's chocolate pudding

Ingredients:

$^1/_2$ litre milk
4 eggs
100 g toasted hazelnuts or 3 teaspoons
hazel paste
8 amaretti macaroons
100 g sugar
$^1/_2$ glass rum
1 tablespoon cocoa powder
Few drops vanilla essence

Method

Crumble the amaretti macaroons into the milk and bring to the boil together with the coffee, rum and vanilla essence. Beat the eggs with the sugar in a separate bowl and add the hazels and cocoa powder. Slowly add the milk and stir constantly for 15 minutes over a low heat with a balloon whisk. Caramelise 2 tablespoons of sugar and put it in the bottom of a pudding mould. Pour in the mixture and steam for 60 minutes. Leave to cool then place in the fridge. Serve cold.

Cream dessert with strawberries

Ingredients:

50 g milk
150 ml fresh cream
50 g sugar
1 stick gelatine
50 g fresh strawberries

Method
Put all the ingredients into a pan and bring to the boil for 10 minutes. Pour into a pudding mould and leave to cool. Place in the fridge for 2 hours before serving.

Turin's 'Gianduiotto' chocolates, now also available in a miniature version called 'Turinot'.

Turin's Al Bicerin Caffé was opened in 1763 by Signor Dentis, sweet-maker and fruit-drink maker, on Royal licence. It is to be found opposite the Sanctuary of the Vergine Consolata. Here, now as many years ago, you can drink the delicious speciality of the house, 'L Bicerin'.

CHOCOLATE*

*T*urin, rightly considered capital city of the
Alps, from the end of the 18th century,
has also been considered 'capital city of chocolate'.
The fame of Turin's chocolate is due to the many
varieties produced there: from chocolate
'bavareisa' to delicious little cups of 'bicerin', a drink
prepared with coffee and chocolate together, the one to
better enhance the flavour of the other, with the addition
of sugar and cream. Chocolate, both milk and plain or
extra bitter, is combined with liqueurs, wines, fruit,
coffee or nuts in a medley of flavours
to suit every palate.
Chocolate: stimulating, nutritious and delightful!

Turin's tradition of chocolate making has lead to the invention
of several types of chocolates which have subsequently risen to
world-wide fame. As far back as 1865 Isidoro Cafferel invented
the 'Gianduiotto' chocolate in the shop founded in Turin by his
French father in 1826. The ingot-shaped Gianduiotto together
with Ferrero's Rocher praline are the area's most-loved products
on a world scale.

The 'Gianduiotto' chocolate was made originally without milk
and contains a fine paste of Piedmontese hazelnuts, the world's
best. The name derives from 'Gianduia', a hero of the
Risorgimento. His original nick-name was Gian d'la Duja,
which in turn derived from Giovanni la Brocca. Giovanni was a
gourmand, a lover of good food and wine. During carnival time
he distributed Caffarel's delicious little pralines which were
immediately named after him.

Over the years, Turin's renowned workshops have invented
innumerable chocolate creations: from pralines and ice-cream to
sculpturesque Easter eggs. In 1826, Brillant Savarin wrote this
verse dedicated to Turin's famous bicerin:

"How happy this chocolate which, from distant shores
(this obviously refers to chocolate's Aztec origins)
finds a woman's smile and melts to death in the
voluptuous kiss of her mouth!"

* The name "bicerin" derives from the delightful little glasses in which this
speciality is still served today.

The Olympic Valley seen from the
Orsiera-Roccavrè Natural Park,
(one of many in Piedmont) near Susa.

PIEDMONTESE HOSPITALITY

HOTELS, VILLAS
AND FAMOUS RESTAURANTS

HOSPITALITY

One of the most pleasurable aspects of a Piedmontese holiday is the hospitality of its inhabitants. A chat with the lady who runs a tiny village shop hidden high up in the hills, with the little old 'contadino' sitting in front of his front door or with the farmer who sells you his wine, cheese or salami will leave a lasting memory of the warmth of these people.

This same simple hospitality is to found in the restaurants and country guest houses which have often been run by the same family for generations and offer a friendly, relaxed atmosphere.

On the other hand, Piedmont also offers a choice of grand hotels fully equipped for international tourism. In our opinion, however, a holiday or short stay in Piedmont is best appreciated in the authentic atmosphere of a family-run concern. Here, the proprietor answers the phone and will settle you in personally, even carrying your bags up to your room himself. The following chapter is dedicated to Piedmont's hotels. We have chosen a small selection of them, situated in villas, castles and ancient buildings, which we consider highly representative of what's on offer.

All of these hotels are comfortable, family-run and romantically atmospheric, perfect for a peaceful sojourn and delightful evenings in their traditionally-run restaurants.

HOTELS & VILLAS

CORTEMILIA - CN (*Alta Langa*)

*V*illa San Carlo

**This modern villa founded and run by the
Zarri family is to be found in Cortemilia,
heart of the Alta Langa region. The Zarris have run
hotels and restaurants for 4 generations.**

Paola is in reception and Carlo will be found in the kitchen.
Everyone does their utmost to ensure the visitor a pleasurable
stay. Villa San Carlo boasts modernised traditional Piedmontese
cuisine served in a cosy candle-lit dining room with 8 tables and
a wood fire, the better to create a romantic and relaxing atmosphere. The wine list has often been acknowledged as being
among the most complete in Italy, with over 1000 varieties to
choose from including many Piedmontese wines and others from
all over the world. From April to October the restaurant's clients
can enjoy the surrounding park complete with swimming pool or
dine in the garden under the stars.

*VILLA SAN CARLO - Corso Divisioni Alpine, 41 - 12074 Cortemilia (CN)
Telephone: +39017381546 - fax. +39017381235
E-mail: info@hotelsancarlo.it - website: www.hotelsancarlo.it*

MONFORTE D'ALBA - CN (Barolo area)

Felicin

This restaurant was founded in 1927
by grandfather Felice. After military service and his
marriage to Claudina he decided to open a restaurant in
Monforte's main square. Now, 70 years on,
it is run by Giorgio and Rosa together with their
young son Felice and his wife, also called Silvia.

A few decades ago Felicin moved to a new location in the
midst of the green Barolo vineyards while still maintaining its
original characteristics of a small, cosy, family-run restaurant.
There are also a small number of guest rooms for those who love
the peace of these beautiful hills.
The cuisine is based on the produce and traditions of the area.
The cellar, one of the region's best, offers a choice of over 700
wines.

ALBERGO - RISTORANTE DA FELICIN
Via Vallada, 18 - 12065 Monforte d'Alba (CN)
Telephone: 0173 78225 - fax 0173 787377
E.mail: albrist@felicin.it - www.felicin.it

POLLENZO - BRA (Cuneo)

ℒa Corte Albertina

The Bertolini family have been expert restauranteurs since 1964 when they opened their famous 'Gallo d'Oro' restaurant in Alba. Following this, they ran the 'Al Castello' restaurant in Santa Vittoria d'Alba (CN). In 1997, Gianni, aided by his parents Enrico and Palmira, opened the 'Corte Albertina' restaurant in Pollenzo.

This historical village, built by King Carlo Alberto of Savoy is also steeped in Roman history: in fact, in Roman times, it was known as 'Pollentia'.

Enrico explains his family's love of fine cooking in the following terms: "Fine cuisine has always been both our family trade and our passion. In order to really get to understand the art of cooking and the secrets of fine wines, you have to share them with friends."

This restaurant has a deep-rooted culture of great cuisine and wines. The cellars boast a wide selection - around 300 - of local wines plus some from abroad selected for the excellent value for money they offer.

LA CORTE ALBERTINA
*Piazza Vittorio Emanuele, 3 - 12060 Fraz. Pollenzo BRA - CN
Telephone and fax 0172 458189*

SANTO STEFANO BELBO - CN (Moscato area)
Relais San Maurizio

**The Relais San Maurizio is situated in one
of the loveliest corners of the Langa area with superb
views over vineyards and castles.**

The building, once a monastery, was later converted into a nobleman's home. Now, from the midst of historical parkland, it offers an air of tranquillity and well-being plus refined pleasures for the palate.

The chef, Guido Alciati and his wife Lidia came from their restaurant, 'Guido', in Costigliole d'Asti, to run the Relais' kitchens. They serve the famous dishes which have brought them renown over the years. In addition, the Relais has a spa centre offering the exclusive method of 'wine therapy'.

There is also a conference centre.

RELAIS SAN MAURIZIO
Località San Maurizio, 39 - 12058 Santo Stefano Belbo (CN)
Telephone: 0141 841900 - fax 0141 843833
E-mail: info@relaissanmaurizio.it
www.relaissanmaurizio.it

CARTOSIO -AL (Acqui Monferrato area)
Cacciatori

Situated in the hills surrounding Acqui Terme,
the Cacciatori restaurant and guest house was founded in
the middle of the 19th century by Francesco Milano,
ancestor of the present-day owners, Giancarlo and Carla.
Francesco ran the village restaurant, known as
'Osteria del Popolo' as well as the village shop, also the
butcher's. He was known locally as 'Radetzky' for his
austere and determined nature.

Today, Carla serves traditional dishes using fresh, seasonal
produce.
Giancarlo and his son Massimo, an expert on Piedmontese
wines, run the dining room. The Milano family also offer the
possibility of a pleasant stay in their comfortably furnished
guest rooms.

CACCIATORI
Via Moreno, 30 - 15015 Cartosio (AL)
Telephone: 0144 40123 - fax 0144 40524

TERRUGGIA - AL (Monferrato Casalese)

Ariotto

This Art- Nouveau style villa was built in the year 1900 by an Italian who had returned home having made his fortune in America. Here, in the green countryside of the Monferrato area, the Garrone family opened their hotel and restaurant, Ariotto, in 1975.

This elegantly-furnished family run concern offers a peaceful atmosphere. Riccardo, the chef, serves a Monferrato-based cuisine while Graziella and son Valerio run the reception and the elegant dining room with its round tables.

The hotel offers all comforts including a swimming pool surrounded by parkland.

HOTEL - RISTORANTE ARIOTTO
Via Prato, 39 - 15030 Terruggia (AL)
Telephone: 0142 402800 - fax 0142 402823
E-mail: info@ariotto.it - www.ariotto.it

VERDUNO - CN (Langhe)
Castello Verduno

Behind Verduno castles's grand front door is a
world from times past. Here, the warmth and cordiality
of the castle-keeper and hotel proprietor, Elisa Burlotto,
and that of her daughters, Alessandra and Elisabetta,
belong to the best of traditions.

The hotel was opened in the castle in 1953 and careful restoration work has recently expanded it into the castle's guest
quarters. The castle's spacious rooms and special atmosphere
are ideally suited to the exhibition of art of all kinds, known as
'Arte nel Castello' ('art in the castle').

The beautifully groomed gardens offer unforgettable
moments of tranquillity with superb views over the Alps and
the surrounding hills. Traditional cuisine from the Langhe is
served in the elegant restaurant.

REAL CASTELLO
Via Umberto I, n° 9 - 12060 Verduno (CN)
Telephone: 0172 470125 - fax 0172 470298
E-mail: castellodiverduno@castellodiverduno.com
www.castellodiverduno.com

COCCONATO - AT (Asti area)

Cannon d'Oro

The Cannon d'Oro restaurant was founded at the end of the 19th century and is situated in the centre of the village of Cocconato d'Asti at 500 metres above sea-level in one of the most scenic places in the area.

Now run by the Tortia family, Paolo the chef and Franca, Maria Grazia and Guido in the dining room will be your hosts. Theirs is a typical Monferrato cuisine accompanied by the best local wines.

The elegant Cannon d'Oro is one of the last truly historical restaurants in the area, family-run for over 100 years. It is still possible today to dine in Prince Umberto of Savoy's favourite room where he used to eat during the 1930s.

The Cannon d'Oro is a must for all lovers of Piedmontese food and also offers the tourist the possibility of a sojourn in its comfortable guest rooms.

HOTEL RISTORANTE
CANNON D'ORO
Piazza Cavour, 21 - 14023 Cocconato (AT)
Telephone: 0141 907794 - fax 0141 907024
E-mail: cannondoro@cannondoro.it - www.cannondoro.it

TORRE PELLICE - TO (Olympic valleys)

$\mathcal{F}$lipot

This restaurant's name derives from that of its
founder in local dialect: Filippo became Flipot.
Founded over 100 years ago, it is now run by Gisella and
Walter Eynard and is famous throughout the country.

Walter took over the restaurant in 1981, marrying Gisella 5
years later. Both true professionals, they describe their love for
their native valley with these words: "it is a unique place with a
unique culture. These mountains are the natural source of many
delights which are subsequently transformed and elaborated
through the craftsmanship of our people."

In 1998 the restaurant was completely restored to its original
18th century beauty, regaining the form of a local farmhouse.

Walter's cuisine is inspired by Waldensian produce and traditions.

FLIPOT
Corso Gramsci, 17 - 10066 Torre Pellice (TO)
Telephone: 0121 953465 - fax 0121 91236
E-mail: flipot@flipot.com - www.flipot.com

ORTA SAN GIULIO - NO (Lakes)

Villa Crespi

*Villa Crespi could have come straight out
of a story from the Arabian Nights.
There are elegant damasks, horseshoe arches
and turquoise ceilings recalling the cupola of a mosque.
What's more, Villa Crespi overlooks
a truly magical place: Lake Orta.*

*Built by Cristoforo Benigno Crespi in 1879 and acquired by
the Marquises Fracassi di Torre Rossano at the end of the 1980s,
it was subsequently transformed into an exclusive 4-star hotel
by the Primatesta family. Run by Cinzia, the daughter of the
family, the hotel and restaurant have become a flower in the
button-hole of Piedmontese hospitality.*

*HOTEL VILLA CRESPI
Via G. Fava 18 - 28016 Orta San Giulio (NO) Lago d'Orta - Italy
Fax +39 0322 911 919 - Telephone: +39 0322 911 902
E-mail: villacrespi@lagodortahotels.com*

CUNEO - CN *(Cuneo area)*

Hotel ristorante Torrismondi

Paolo Rosa belongs to the third generation of restaurant owners to run the Torrismondi restaurant in the centre of Cuneo.

This is a small tastefully -furnished restaurant. An interesting feature is the collection of antique prints depicting various gastronomic delights, especially those of the Cuneo area.

Tradition, but also imagination and a pinch of daring, are Torrismondi's key words. The atmosphere is familial with Paolo's mum Irma and his wife Patrizia to welcome you in.

Pippi (Paolo) and Pacci (Patrizia) have great faith in local produce.

Their dishes, wines and cheeses reflect this fact. Adjacent to the restaurant is a comfortable, 25-room hotel.

HOTEL RISTORANTE TORRISMONDI
Via Michele Coppino, 33 - Cuneo
Telephone: 0171 630861 - fax 0171 443267

RESTAURANTS

In addition to the hotels already mentioned, the following is a list of choice restaurants which can be enjoyed during one or more of the various tours described further on in the book.

All these restaurants are family-run and offer cuisine and warm hospitality typical of the region.

MONTELUPO ALBESE - CN (Alta Langa area)
*R*istorante Ca' del Lupo

*Situated on one of the hills around Montelupo,
a village near Alba with medieval origins,
the Cà del Lupo restaurant offers splendid views
of the Alps through its picture windows.*

*During the summer months guests can dine in the garden,
making the most of the refreshing hill-climate. All ingredients
are selected for their freshness and often produce from local
farms is used. There is a wood oven where delicious bread,
'focaccia' and breadsticks are prepared and which is also used
for cooking of certain specialities of the house. All dishes are
prepared in the Cà del Lupo kitchens following traditional recipes of the region.*

RISTORANTE CÀ DEL LUPO,
via Ballerina, 15 - 12050 Montelupo Albese (CN)
Telephone: 0173 617249 - fax 0173 617249
E-mail: cadellupo@cadellupo.it

COSSANO - CN *(Alta Langa and Moscato area)*

$\mathscr{T}$rattoria della Posta da Camulin

*There is a family atmosphere at Camulin's which was
once a post-house with adjoining stables.
Many years have passed since the men of the
postal service and their horses stayed here but
the delicious recipes of almost a century and a half ago
are still prepared in Camulin's kitchens.*

Today, the restaurant is run by Giorgio Giordano and his
family. Cesare, a professional sommelier runs the dining room
and mamma Giovanna the kitchens. The founder, Giorgio's
grandfather, came from the nearby village of Camo and was
nick-named 'Camulin', 'little Camillo', for his short stature.

TRATTORIA DELLA POSTA DA CAMULIN
Via Fratelli Negro, 3 - 12054 Cossano Belbo (CN)
Telephone: 0141 88126 - fax 0141 88559

BENEVELLO - ALBA (CN)

Relais Villa d'Amelia

*'Nonna', Grandma, Amelia will live again after
the restoration of the house that she once reigned over is
complete. Lorenzo, Amelia's direct descendent,
is personally overseeing all the work being done at
Cascina Borelli in the hamlet of Manera near Alba.*

The restaurant is due to open in 2005 and will be known as 'Villa d'Amelia', a relais with an 18th century, family-run atmosphere situated in parkland of over 70,000 square metres. Surrounded by hazel groves and woodlands, the relais will boast breathtaking views over the Monviso Alpine range and the Barolo vineyards.

The original farmhouse, or cascina, owned by Amelia Bonelli Bianchi,was built in 1858. Once restored, it will offer all comforts for the guest who wants to relax in style and enjoy the delights of excellent cuisine and wines in truly romantic and fascinating surroundings. The nearby chapel, complete with 18th century frescoes, is also being accurately restored.

RISTORANTE VILLA D'AMELIA
Località Manera - Benevello (CN)
Telephone 0173 529225 - fax 0173 529278
E-mail: info@villadamelia.it

MONFORTE - CN (Barolo area)

Trattoria della Posta

The Trattoria della Posta preserves antique traditions, hospitality and character while offering the type of high-quality service which is suited to the modern-day tourist.

Gianfranco, the chef-proprietor, is an expert on local produce and the best way to prepare it. There is a monumental wine list including many important local crus.

This is an elegant but not overly-sophisticated restaurant which just has to be experienced!

TRATTORIA DELLA POSTA
Località Sant'Anna, 87 - 12065 Monforte d'Alba (CN)
Telephone: 0173 78120 - fax 0173 78120

BARBARESCO - CN *(Barbaresco and Alba area)*

*R*istorante Rabayà

This restaurant was founded in 1989 in the
heart of one of the most prestigious areas of the
Barbaresco zone, from it derives its name.
With its wide red-brick arches, its wooden beams
and its antique furniture, the Rabayà offers
an atmosphere which is both elegant
and rustic - suited to lovers of traditional Langa cuisine.

Typical dishes include tasty starters, home-made pasta and
the Rabayà classic, rabbit cooked in Barbaresco. The wine-list is
rich and varied, containing over 600 varieties. Hundreds of bottles wait patiently in the Rabayà's cellars for the day in which
they will be uncorked in front of the wood fire in winter or on
the lovely terrace in summer where you can admire the sun as
it sets behind the hills.

RISTORANTE RABAJÀ
Via Rabajà, 9 - 12050 Barbaresco (CN)
Telephone: 0173 635223 - fax 0173 635226
E-mail: rabaya@tiscalinet.it

TREISO - CN *(Barbaresco and Alba area)*

La Ciau del Tornavento

At only 7 kilometres from Alba,
the village of Treiso is in the heart of the Barbaresco
region, where the hills converge with one another,
capturing the sun's rays. Nadia Benech and Maurilio
Garola practice their art here, taking inspiration
from this bountiful land.

Their cuisine is traditional with a touch of originality and
imagination. The restaurant is furnished in an elegant but traditional fashion. There are 2 comfortable and relaxing dining
rooms and a splendidly green garden for use in the summer
months with beautiful views. It is possible to savour an aperitif
or liqueur in the cellars while admiring the many wines on
display there, mostly the produce of local vintners although
wines from the rest of Italy and the world are included.

LA CIAU DEL TORNAVENTO
Piazza Baracco, 7 - 12050 Treiso (CN)
Telephone: 0173 638333 - fax 0173 638352

CASALE - AL *(Casale and Vercelli area)*

*R*istorante La Torre

This restaurant, founded in 1966, is situated
on the hill which dominates the town of Casale
Monferrato within a villa-cum-castle
in the midst of greenery.

The views over the neighbouring hills of the Monferrato area
and to the river Po and beyond, are splendid. The Torre is one
of the most traditional Piedmontese restaurants where you will
be able to enjoy refined cuisine based on local produce carefully chosen by the cook, Patrizia Grossi, in elegantly-furnished
dining rooms. The cellars contain a wide variety of both Italian
and foreign wines with particular regard to new producers.

...This is an angle of the Monferrato which offers unforgettable moments!

RISTORANTE LA TORRE
Via Diego Garoglio, 3 - 15033 Casale Monferrato (AL)
Telephone: 0142 70295 - fax 0142 70295

MURISENGO - AL (Casale area)

Cascina Martini

Gianluigi Giachino and his wife Mariangela have restored to its former glory this 19th century farmhouse which had belonged to the family for many years.

In what used to be the farm's stables they have opened their restaurant with its elegantly rustic atmosphere. Outside there is a peaceful garden where it is possible to dine during the summer months.

The cuisine is entirely based on local produce with a touch of imagination and for few guests only. In the refurbished cellars wine, cheese and salami tasting sessions are organised.

The wine list is also certainly worth perusing.

RISTORANTE CASCINA MARTINI
Via Gianoli, 15 - 15020 Murisengo (AL)
Telephone: 0141 693015 - fax 0141 693015
E-mail: cascinamartini@cascinamartini.com.

ACQUI TERME- AL (Alessandria Monferrato area)
$\mathcal{R}$istorante La Schiavia

The La Schiavia restaurant is to be found
on the way up to Acqui Terme's splendid cathedral. This
restaurant, owned by Roberto Abrile, is situated in a late
17th century nobleman's house, refurbished with style
and elegance while maintaining moulded
plaster ceilings and period furniture.

The cuisine is adventurous and tasty, combining elements of
Ligurian cooking with Piedmontese traditions. Among the starters you will find 'filetto baciato' and peppers Parmesan gratiné
with capers and anchovies. First courses are very varied, including ravioli with fondue, pasta and beans and tagliatelle with
truffle and robiola cheese from Roccaverano. Meat dishes include rabbit cooked with herbs, Schiavia fillet steak and stockfish
Acqui style. There is a high-quality wine list with 350 varieties
among the best Italian and French crus.

RISTORANTE LA SCHIAVIA
Vicolo Della Schiavia - 15011 Acqui Terme (AL)
Telephone/Fax: 0144 55939

ASTI - AT (Asti Monferrato area)

Il Convivio Vini e Cucina

The Il Convivio Vini e Cucina restaurant was founded in 1986 in a period building, subsequently refurbished, situated in the historical centre of Asti.

The cuisine is inspired by local traditions with particular regard for Piedmontese cheeses and seasonal produce. The wines are Italian, mainly from Piedmont and in particular the Asti area. An atmosphere of warm hospitality and professionalism is ensured by the restaurant's youthful staff: Carmen Montanaro in the kitchen and Giuliano Borello and Danilo Machetti in the dining room.

There is also a restored period wine cellar which can be visited.

IL CONVIVIO VINI E CUCINA
Via G.B. Giuliani , 6 - 14100 Asti (AT)
Telephone: 0141 594188 - fax 0141 594188

MONTEMAGNO - AT (Asti Monferrato area)

*R*istorante La Braja

Antonio and Giuseppe Palermino have run this restaurant with professionalism and originality since 1975.

Situated in the midst of the Asti Monferrato hills within the village of Montemagno, dominated by its aristocratic castle, this restaurant is perfect for lovers of haute cuisine. The excellent dishes proposed by the Palermino brothers, now aided in their work by their sons Ezio and Christian, are accompanied by a wide range of wines from Piedmont and beyond.

RISTORANTE LA BRAJA
Via San Giovanni Bosco 11 14030 Montemagno AT
Telephone: 0141 653925   FAX: 0141 63605

CANALE - CN (Roero)
Ristorante Enoteca

The Enoteca restaurant is situated in the heart of the Roero, the area which joins the Monferrato to the Langhe, and its cuisine reflects this combination.

The vast menu contains dishes with rural 'contadino' origins embellished with refined innovations added by the local aristocracy and bourgeoisie, the rich merchant classes. The dining room is luminous and comfortable with period furnishings in perfect harmony with the building. The cellars offer all the wines selected by the Enoteca del Roero (local Wine Centre) plus other prestigious wines. Davide Palluda, the chef, employs the skills acquired in some of the finest restaurants in both Piedmont and Liguria. His sister Ivana runs the dining room.

RISTORANTE ENOTECA
Via Roma, 57 - 12043 Canale (CN)
Telephone: 0173 95857 - fax 0173 95857

SANTA VITTORIA - CN (Roero)

Ristorante del Castello

*Situated in the heart of an ancient castle,
this hotel and restaurant offer peace and tranquillity.
The views from the terrace over the hills of the
Roero and Langhe and the ancient tower
take you back to times past.*

A famous novel and film 'The Secret of Santa Vittoria' tell the story of how the inhabitants of the village hid their greatest treasure, their wine, in grottos beneath the hills to save it from theft. These days, the treasures of the area may be tasted in the dining rooms and the wines are no longer hidden away but shine as bright as the moon in their scintillating glasses. The Castello restaurant offers recipes from times past including Alba's truffles, wild mushrooms and the noble wines of the Roero and Langhe areas.

RISTORANTE DEL CASTELLO
Via Cagna, 4 - 12069 Santa Vittoria (CN)
Telephone: 0172 478198 - fax 0172 478465

TORINO - TO

Ristorante Cantina Babette

In the heart of Turin, at just a stone's throw from Piazza San Carlo, this new restaurant is to be found. Built within a prestigious 17th century baroque palace, Cantina Babette possesses an originally modern design, linear and elegant furnishings and is distributed throughout various levels of the palace offering rooms of various sizes. The manager, Antonio Dacomo and the chef, Claudio Boretto have great ambitions for their restaurant.

The cuisine is classical in style with creative and original touches. Alessandro Pegoraro, pastry chef, adds fascination with his creations. The restaurant's cellar, known as the 'wine tower' is certainly the restaurant's focal point. The tower is built in wood and glass and contains over 6000 bottles positioned horizontally. It is so designed that all the bottles may be reached without the use of a ladder.

The wine list is a sort of encyclopaedia which, in addition to offering the list itself, also provides information on the wines it contains. The experienced staff's aim is to ensure that clients are completely at ease.

RISTORANTE CANTINA BABETTE
Via Alfieri, 16/B - 10121 Torino (TO)
Telephone 011 547882 - fax 011 19503412
www.ristorantebabette.it - E-mail: postmaster@ristorantebabette.it

RIVOLI - TO

*R*istorante Combal.Zero

*This restaurant is considered a reference
point of the area, situated at the mouth
of the Susa valley not far from Turin.*

It is to be found in the long wing of the 18th century Rivoli castle, once home of the Sabauda dynasties, which now also houses the museum of contemporary art. The restaurant has gained Michelin stars for its cuisine, never run-of-the-mill, always open to innovation. Here, eating becomes an all-encompassing experience.

Davide Scabin, the creative chef, chooses his ingredients with the greatest of care, then builds up each flavour adding exactly the right dose of imagination. The carte offers 4 main types of menu: classical cuisine, local cooking, creative cuisine and bar-restaurant.

The wine list offers 600 painstakingly selected labels.

RISTORANTE COMBAL.ZERO
Piazza Mafalda di Savoia, - 10098 Rivoli (TO)
Telephone 011 9565225 - fax 011 9565238
E-mail: combal.zero@combal.org

TURIN - TO

$\mathcal{R}$istorante 'L Birichin

*Nicola Batavia, the proprietor, is the 'Birichin'
('cheeky boy') of the restaurant's name.
He interprets Piedmontese cuisine in the comfortable
atmosphere of his restaurant and includes
fish on the menu.*

*The excellent wine list which accompanies the house speciali-
ties tempts the palate.*

RISTORANTE 'L BIRICHIN
Via V. Monti, 16/a - 10126 Torino (TO)
Telephone: 011 657457 - fax 011 657457

Before the scientists in their white coats
offer us
factory-made 'vitello tonnato' or freeze-dried
'fritto misto' or a pre-cooked
'finanziera' (just re-heat),
before they propose we drink a good vintage
aluminium-packed
and reduced to a convenient powder
to dissolve in water before consumption,
let's all sit down to a real meal,
the sort that has always been served
in these parts- who knows?
It could be our last!

Gigi Marsico

There's a kind of sun on these hill-tops, a vibration of chalky rocks and crickets that I'd forgotten about. Here, the heat doesn't seem to descend from the sky so much as arise from the earth, from the furrows between the vines. The heat seems to have eaten up all the greenness and sent it into the vine shoots.

"It's a heat I like, it has an odour: I'm in this odour too, together with harvests and hay-makings and prunings — so many flavours and desires I didn't know I had in me. So I liked to come out of the Angel to keep an eye on the countryside..."

"The Moon and the Bonfires"
by Cesare Pavese

TOURS TO ENJOY

ALTA LANGA AREA
THE BAROLO AND BARBARESCO HILLS
THE MOSCATO TOUR
THE ROERO AREA
THE ASTI MONFERRATO AREA
THE ALESSANDRIA MONFERRATO AREA
THE CUNEO AREA
THE CASALE AREA AND VERCELLI RICE
THE LAKES
THE SABAUDA RESIDENCES
THE OLYMPIC VALLEYS

ITINERARIES

Piedmont is one of the regions of Italy with the richest historical and artistic heritage.
Hilly topography, temperate climate and richness of terrain have all contributed to its position at the top of fruit and cereal crop production on a world scale.
Many products are unique to the area.

The following tours aim to give some idea of this region as yet undiscovered by mass tourism where nature and traditions are jealously conserved by the inhabitants.

There are trails which take you through noble plantations of fruit and vegetables, along woodland paths scented with wild mushrooms, truffles and game and past hills dominated by their castles and towers, tangible signs of Piedmont's past.

There are isolated hill-top villages undisturbed by time to discover, and village festivals and fairs which keep traditions and ancient ways of life alive. These are the sensations which we hope to impart to the visitor to Piedmont.

These itineraries are only an indication of the most important sites and other features. Similarly, the routes are indicative. For more detailed guides we would advise consulting one of the area's tourist information offices.

From my own personal experience, I would advise planning a route along one of the trails indicated either by car or bike. Get ready to discover unforgettable places!

The Langa in winter:
a most beautiful sight and a time of repose for local folk.

ALTA LANGA ITINERARY

The Alta Langa area is probably the wildest part of Piedmont. Its extraordinary landscape alternates oak and chestnut woods with groves of the world's most prestigious hazelnuts.
There are terraced vineyards, fallow land for grazing and cultivated fields.

This is a land which jealously conserves its traditions, dedicated more to nature and its products than to tourism.

Our tour commences at **Cortemilia**. This is the largest village in the nearby valleys and is famous as the centre of production for the 'Tonda Gentile delle Langhe' hazelnut which has obtained the 'IGP Piedmont' denomination. We advise a stroll through its 2 centres and a visit to the Romanesque church as a start to the tour.

First call is **Valle Uzzone** with a visit to the castle of Gorrino and the Todocco Sanctuary. On your return, in the comune of Pezzolo, a little metalled road will take you up to **Bergolo**, 'village of stone', one of the prettiest villages in the area. It is composed of a small number of stone-built houses decorated with frescoes by young artists from all over the world.

The tour continues along the crest of the hill with a beautiful view towards **Levice and Prunetto**. Here, at a height of 750 m above sea-level there is the Scarampi castle to visit, built around the year 1000 and now the site of an interesting museum.

Now it is time to descend towards **Monesiglio** to take the panoramic road for **Mombarcaro and Niella Belbo**, a road which seems to take you over the top of the world, finally leading through hazel groves towards Feisoglio, Cravanzana, Torre Bormida and back to Cortemilia.

BAROLO ITINERARY

*This journey starts at **Monforte** and proceeds towards the village of **Barolo** for a visit to the castle of the Falletti family of Barolo which houses a museum of viticulture. The castle is also home to the regional Wine Centre ('Enoteca') with examples of all major producers of this noble wine.*

*Now the road takes you through prestigious vineyards towards the village of **La Morra** where a visit to the panoramic Belvedere, on the top of the hill, is mandatory. From here an incomparable view of the hills and the Maritime Alps can be enjoyed.*

*The second part of the tour is dedicated to a visit to the **castle of Grinzane Cavour**, once the residence of Count Camillo Benso, the politician who brought about the unification of Italy and which now houses a museum documenting his life. Today, the castle is also the site of a museum of antique country crafts and the regional Wine Centre of Piedmont.*

*At **Sinio**, a little village a few kilometres away there is a typical Langa 'torronificio', or nougat factory, which is worth a visit. On the way back to **Monforte**, you pass through **Castiglione Falletto** with its castle dating back to the year 1001, once a military fortress and now, with its fortifications, a tourist attraction.*

The rest of the journey is a feast for the eyes. We would advise at least one stop off at a producer of Barolo along the way.

*Alba: the spectacular church of San Domenico dating back to
1292 with its portal depicting the Virgin Mary presenting the
Christ child to Saint Domenico and Saint Catherine.
The lovely main portal with its columns of sandstone
and coloured bands of brick is not to be missed.*

BARBARESCO ITINERARY

*Our tour starts at Neive,
situated on the top of a hill.
There are cobbled lanes to stroll through while admiring
the ancient buildings, such as palazzo Cocito,
palazzo Bongioanni and palazzo Borgese and other
attractive stone-built houses typical of the Langa.
The late baroque parish church of Saints
Peter and Paul is worth a visit with
its 18th century stuccoes.*

The excursion continues through the hills of Barbaresco.

The first stop is **Mango** with its castle built on the foundations of a 13th century fortress which now houses the regional Wine Centre for Moscato d'Asti and Piedmontese sparkling wines in general.

The tour continues towards **Barbaresco** along the road flanked by vineyards where the homonymous vines are grown. The magnificent view to be had from the top of the village is truly breathtaking. The regional Wine Centre for Barbaresco is situated in the deconsecrated church of San Donato and the best wines of the local area are to be found within.

A few kilometres away lies the town of **Alba**, also known as 'the town of a 100 towers', with its 'centro storico'. The main street, Via Vittorio Emanuele, also known as 'Via Maestra', is full of elegant shops and historical caffès, offering the chance to shop and relax at the same time. We advise a visit to the meeting room of the 'Municipio' (town hall) to see the paintings and frescoes, including a late 14th century crucifixion. The cathedral of San Lorenzo is a Romanesque-Gothic building with an interesting 16th century wooden choir stall. **San Domenico and 'La Maddalena'** are other interesting churches in the town centre.

The return journey to Neive takes you along the Alba-Asti road as far as Castagnito where a left turn takes you onto the Neive road. A visit to one or more of the Barbaresco wineries is a must.

In his last novel, ('The Moon and the Bonfires', 1950), Cesare Pavese often refers to his friend and advisor Nuto, (Pino Scaglino). He also talks of music and one of the dialogues reads: "Nuto noticed that they'd seen and said immediately. I'll tell you a story.
They had a musician, Arboreto, who played the bugle..."

MOSCATO ITINERARY

This tour starts at **Santo Stefano Belbo**,
*birthplace of the writer Cesare Pavese, and proceeds
along the classical 'Moscato roads' of the literary park
dedicated to him. At Santo Stefano it is possible to visit
the house where Pavese was born, the Cesare Pavese
study centre and the house-museum of Nuto, the main
character in Pavese's most famous novel,*
'The Moon and the Bonfires'.

On the way along the Belbo valley towards **Cossano Belbo**,
we advise a stop at the 'Antico Mulino', the old mill, belonging
to the Marino family, where the millstone can still be seen. On
your way out of the village on the left, a scenic road takes you
up to the village of **Castino** via the hamlet of **Scorrone**. The
view over a series of hills, each with its castle or tower, is splendid. In the past, these fortifications served to warn of the arrival of enemy armies. Here, it is possible to admire the **towers
of Perletto**, **San Giorgio Scarampi and Roccaverano** and,
on the right, the ruins of the castle of **Cortemilia**. Now, the
main road takes you through the Bormida valley in the direction
of Acqui Terme. All of the little villages which can be seen from
this road are worth a visit and their streets full of flowers and
history are the ideal place for a peaceful stroll.

From **Roccaverano**, the tour continues to **Monastero
Bormida** where there is an imposing Benedictine monastery
built during the 9th and 10th centuries. It is possible to visit the
monastery which also houses a museum.

Bubbio is only 5 kilometres away and is famous for its DOC
and DOCG wines and also for being one of the first anti-tran-
sgenic comunes in Italy. Here, Arbiora matures and sells the
famous 'Roccaverano' cheese. The road now proceeds for
Canelli via the Caffi Sanctuary.

Canelli is a little town which is famous for its historical
Spumante wineries. A pleasant walk along a road cobbled with
river pebbles takes you from the historical centre to the castle
belonging to the Gancia family. From here, the lovely view over
the Monferrato hills and the town can be admired before the
return journey to Santo Stefano Belbo.

An old house in Magliano Alfieri with attractive examples of local plasterwork in the fireplace and ceiling.

ROERO ITINERARY

This tour starts from Verduno for the castle of Magliano Alfieri passing along the main Alba-Bra road and following the indications for Santa Vittoria, Monticello and Castellinaldo. The route winds along the lanes of the white wine area where Arneis and Favorita are produced.

The **Magliano Alfieri castle** is 18th century and houses a museum of art and traditions of the Roero area, including a plaster cast museum. The view from the castle grounds is wonderful. Not far from here is the village of **Govone** with another beautiful, baroque, castle which was once part of the Sabauda residences (see p 250). The manor gardens were designed by the famous architect Guarino Guarini and now host art exhibitions and conferences.

The tour continues to **Canale** where it is possible to visit the regional Wine Centre. In the afternoon we advise a visit to **Bra** where the baroque church of Sant'Andrea and the Palazzo Traversa museum of art and history which contains an archeological collection from nearby Pollenzo (the Roman Pollentia) can be admired. Piazza della Rocca and Via Cavour contain elegant shops and caffès.

A few minutes from Bra is the town of **Cherasco**, a town with Roman origins. Worth visiting is the Palazzo Salmatoris where Napoleon Bonaparte stayed and which now houses a much-appreciated gallery of modern art, both Piedmontese and international.

The collegiate church of San Secondo, the much-loved patron saint who was a soldier and warrior. The church is known as the 'church of the Saint' or 'el Sant, in local dialect, by the people of Asti.

ASTI MONFERRATO ITINERARY

Our day out can commence with a visit to the historical centre of Asti. The city was founded by the Ligurians in the year 500 B.C and was dominated successively by the Romans, the Longobards and the Franks until the year 1095 A.D when it acquired its independence.

The tour starts at the church **Collegiata di San Secondo** (1327 - 1354), the oldest church in Asti. It is possible to visit the late 6th century crypt where the body of Saint Secondo, patron saint of Asti was preserved until 1597. Via Alfieri, dedicated to Asti's most famous tragedy, is the main street of Asti which, in addition to numerous shops also contains the synagogue and Jewish museum, the Alfieri museum and study centre contained within the 13th century Alfieri palace, the 13th century Troiana tower in Romanesque Ghibelline style and the 15th century Malabaila palace.

At the end of the main street there is the Roman **Torre Rossa** where Saint Secondo is supposed to be have been held prisoner. The cathedral is in the Piedmontese Gothic style and was built during the 14th century by local masters with French architectural and decorative inspiration.

After the visit to Asti we advise a tour of the Barbera hills to **Costigliole d'Asti** to visit the castle and then on to **Nizza Monferrato**, home of the Nizza cardoon, where you can enjoy a stroll through the 'centro storico' and a coffee. Finally, just north of Asti is **Castelnuovo Don Bosco** birthplace of Don Bosco, founder of the Salesian order.

The 'boiling fountain' ('La bollente') of spa water at Acqui Terme.

The parish church of San Giacomo at Gavi: the great painting by Gandolfino Da Roreto, recently restored with funds donated by the Lions Club.

ALESSANDRIA MONFERRATO ITINERARY

*A good idea is to start this tour with a visit to the spa town of **Acqui Terme**. First stop is the central Piazza Italia with the elegant Ninfee (water lily) fountain. A stroll through Corso Italia, the shopping street, will take you past the '**Bollente**' a fountain of spa water at 75°c which is worth investigating.*

Towards Corso Bagni, the **cathedral of Saint Guido** can be visited every day except Sunday. It is a Romanesque building and contains the Bermejo triptych, a work by the famous Spanish 15th century painter. Here you can also see the archeological site of the Roman baths discovered right beneath the archway of the street.

In the late morning you can continue towards **Ovada** along scenic hills on top of which can be seen the towers of Cremolino, Prasco and Morsasco. Ovada has an interesting historical centre with obvious Genoese influences. Worth seeing are the churches of Santa Maria delle Grazie and dell'Assunta.

From Ovada, continue towards **Gavi** which gives its name to the great Piedmontese dry white wine world-renowned for its bouquet and perfumes. We advise a visit to the fortress of Gavi and to one or more of the local wineries for a tasting session and a snack of some tasty local dish.

Hot air balloons float over Cuneo.

CUNEO ITINERARY

Our Cuneo tour starts in the valley most famous
*for its chestnuts, **the valle Pesio**.*

After you have visited the historical centre of Chiusa Pesio it is well worth making a detour to visit the natural beauty of the nearby valleys. For example, you can take the road to the Certosa di Pesio, a monastery at 900m above sea level situated at the beginning of the Alta Valle Pesio park. The monastery, a closed order, was founded by Saint Brunone in 1173 and possesses a Romanesque church, reconstructed during the Renaissance period. It is surrounded by chestnut and beech woods and comprises 2 cloisters. Enjoyable walks through the woods in close contact with nature may be taken throughout the valley.

Other interesting excursions around Cuneo are to the **Valgrana** and **Stura valleys**. The former is renowned for Castelmagno, its famous cheese and its meadows and the latter for its scenic road which leads up to the thermal baths at Vinadio and the village of Pietraporzio.

Certosa di Pesio

The chapel of the Sanctuary of the 'Sacro Monte' at Crea.

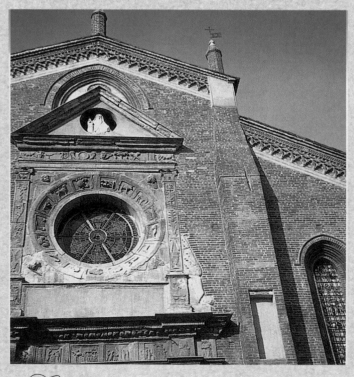

Casale Monferrato: the church of San Domenico.

CASALE AND VERCELLI RICE ITINERARY

*The tour starts with a visit to the historical centre of **Casale Monferrato**. From elegant Piazza Mazzini, locally known as 'piazza del cavallo' (horse square) because of its equestrian statue, you proceed to the Romanesque cathedral dedicated to Saint Evasio. The interior possesses 5 naves plus a rare narthex. Also of note is Sannazzaro palace with its elaborate balcony and scenic courtyard, Gozzani di Treville palace, which was originally 18th century, and Casa Tornelli, with its fine Gothic architecture.*

During the latter part of the morning we advise a trip to **Serralunga di Crea** to visit the park established by the Region of Piedmont in 1980 to protect the natural and architectural treasures found there. In fact, within the park is the **Sacro Monte** (sacred mount) of Crea, with 23 chapels forming a Via Crucis. The most impressive is the Cappella del Paradiso (paradise chapel) dedicated to the coronation of the Virgin Mary.

During the afternoon, our tour takes us through the world's most prestigious rice fields, those of Vercelli. Starting at Trino Vercellese you proceed to Desana where we advise a stop at the 'Tenuta Castello' farm, rice producers for over 100 years. Here, the varieties Carnaroli, Vialone, Arborio etc are all cultivated.

THE LAKES

*Itinerary: From Lake Maggiore to Lake Orta Stresa
Mottarone - Orta San Giulio - San Maurizio d'Opaglio
Omegna Valle Strona - Tecnoparco del Lago Maggiore
Baveno - Stresa*

The tour starts at **Stresa** with a visit to its beautiful villas.
The 18th century Villa Ducale possesses gardens containing
the rare 'Magnolia Grandiflora'. Others to see are: Villa
Bolongaro, now a Rosminian college with monuments to
Rosmini, and Villa Pallavicino, with its zoo and park. You can
then proceed to the islands of **Isola Bella, Isola Madre** and
Isola Pescatori by motorboat.

By car, we advise a trip to the scenic point of Mottarone
(1,491 above sea level) and the Alpinia gardens. From
Mottarone you descend towards Armeno and Miasino to visit
Villa Nigra. We also advise a stop at Vacciago di Ameno
(Museum foundation Calderara) and **Ameno** (the Villa Monte
Oro park). Once you are at Lake Orta you will want to visit the
Sacro Monte di Orta. The town of Orta has a square facing
the island of **San Giulio**, which contains the Palazzo
Comunale, dating from 1582, balancing on its portico and
many baroque houses and palaces, such as Villa Bossi, now the
town hall, Palazzo Gemelli and Villa Motta. The island of San
Giulio with its homonymous Romanesque basilica needs to be
seen, including the 12th century crypt and pulpit. Casa Tallone
is worth a visit. Having left Orta, the road takes you along the
south bank dominated by the rocks of Madonna del Sasso. At
San Maurizio d'Opaglio there is the Museum of the Tap to
see before leaving for **Omegna**, an industrial centre where household goods are made, situated on the banks of the lake and possessing a frescoed 13th century parish church. A detour to **Valle
Strona** is worth while to see the Museum of Wind Instruments
of Quarna. Having then returned to Omegna, you can proceed
towards Gravellona Toce and Lake Maggiore. We advise stop-
ping at the futuristic Tecnoparco del Lago Maggiore before pro-
ceeding to the picturesque village of Feriolo.

At **Feriolo** you follow the signs for **Baveno**, a little tourist
spot famed for its pink granite quarries and attractive lakeside
area. Here, the parish church has a Romanesque facade and bell-
tower. There are 15th century frescoes to be seen inside the baptistery. Also of note is the Fedora park.

A lovely view of the island of San Giulio in the midst of the waters of Lake d'Orta in the Novara area.

Isola Bella island in Lake Maggiore.

The castle of Govone, province of Cuneo. The young Rousseau stayed in this scenic royal palace in 1730. At that time it still belonged to Count Ottavio Solaro di Govone. From 1792 to 1870 it was property of the Savoy dynasty. It is now the local town hall.

Pollenzo (Bra): the neo-gothic church of San Vittore belonging to the royal hunting estate. Like others, including Racconigi, Govone and La Mandria, King Carlo Alberto subsequently transformed, the area into a farming estate.

THE SABAUDA RESIDENCES

As was mentioned on pages 25 and 26, the residences of the Sabauda Court are Piedmontese architectural gems protected by Unesco as part of world heritage.

These magnificent palaces and castles in ancient parkland were built by the Savoy Royal family over the last few centuries of Piedmontese history.

Of the 14 most interesting, 5 are to be found in the city of Turin: Palazzo Reale, Palazzo Madama, Palazzo Carignano, Villa della Regina and the Valentino castle. Another 6 are to be found in the immediate vicinity of the city: the castle of Moncalieri, the castle of Stupinigi, the castle of Rivoli, Palazzo Reale di Venaria, the castle of La Mandria and the castle of the Duchy of Agliè. Three are to be found to the south of Turin towards the Langa region: the castle of Racconigi, the castle of Pollenzo and the castle of Govone.

While the Turin palaces can easily be visited during a tour of the city, a car is necessary to visit the others. One day could be spent visiting the castles of Moncalieri, Stupinigi and Rivoli, for example and another dedicated to the delights of the Venaria park, the castle of La Mandria and the castle of the Duchy of Agliè.

The castle of Racconigi can be visited if an excursion to the Langa and Roero district is being contemplated. Those of Govone and Pollenzo are to be found in the Roero area.

Museums, paintings, lovely stuccoes, collections of antique objects: art and history in general, are the attractions which each of these fascinating buildings offers. In addition, some are also surrounded by stupendous parkland which was used by past kings for their hunting activities. Delightful walks can be enjoyed through these parks to admire the flora and fauna they contain in an uncontaminated environment.

FOR FURTHER INFORMATION CONTACT THE TOURIST OFFICE:
Ufficio Turistico "Turismo Torino", piazza Castello, 161 - Torino
Telephone: 011 535181 - fax. 011 530070 - www.turismotorino.org

The Royal Palace, Turin

Madama Palace, Turin

Stupinigi Castle

Venaria Royal Palace

*Villa della Regina
Turin*

Racconigi Castle

Rivoli Castle

Moncalieri Castle

THE OLYMPIC VALLEYS

*From Turin, city of the Olympic Games,
you enter into the Susa valley with
its medieval atmosphere.
In fact, at Avigliana, the medieval town
centre is intact with its towers and steeples
outlined against the nearby hill.
Not far from here, Precettoria di Sant'Antonio
possesses elegant terracotta pinnacles.*

To get to the **Sacra di San Michele**, symbol of Piedmont and austere on the top of its mountain, you travel along the banks of the morainic lake Avigliana. From here, you travel to the top of Mount Pirchiano, where, it is said, the Archangel Michael once appeared. The monastery developed during the 11th century from 3 chapels built within the rock. On top of these were built the basilica and other abbey buildings. To get to the monastery, you have to climb the steep 'Salone dei Morti' or 'Room of the Dead' dug through the rock. At the top, there is the beautiful 12th century 'Portale dello Zodiaco' or 'Zodiac Door', the work of Master Nicolò. From the terrace a magnificent view over Turin can be admired. Our journey proceeds along the valley to **Susa**. This town, built on the banks of the Doria Riparia river, was once considered the 'door to Italy' for its strategic position between Moncenisio and Monginevro. The castle of the Marquisa Adelaide, 10th century founder of the Savoy dynasty, dominates the town. The most famous building is the cathedral of Saint Giusto with its splendid Romanesque steeple and the adjacent Porta Savoia, erected over 3rd-century-B.C. Roman foundations. Once through this door, you find yourself in a maze of little medieval lanes with covered walkways known as 'Borgo dei Nobili'.

The tour continues to **Exilles** where the fortress, until 1713, represented the confines of the Dauphinate and was also a much-feared prison. Among its prisoners was the mysterious 'Man in the Iron Mask'. **Bardonecchia** was the first skiing resort and, in 1909, held the very first national competition for

Historical skis and attachments from the collection of the Ravelli brothers, Turin

Bardonecchia 1909
The contestants Cristina Silvetti and Ottavia and Enrica Dumontel of the Turin Ski Club, the first of its kind in Italy

female skiers. Past **Sestriere**, *the famous ski resort where the 2006 Alpine skiing competitions will be held, you reach* **Pragelato**. *Here, you can take a stroll among its 18 hamlets to admire the typical architecture of the Chisone valley. This is the ideal place to taste and acquire local products, such as those of Albergian - the Genepy, fruit jams and so on. There is also a recently founded ethnographical museum with typical local costumes and agricultural implements.*

Further along the valley you arrive at **Fenestrelle** *with its imposing fortress, known as* **'The Great Wall of Piedmont'**. *Building was started by Vittorio Amedeo II in 1728 although only part of the wall was completed. Subsequently, Carlo Alberto finished the construction of the wall which, in all, had lasted a total of 122 years. It is a military structure in brick and stone and unique in the whole of Europe for its size (1,300,000 metres squared in all, it contains a covered stairway with over 4000 steps).*

FOR FURTHER INFORMATION:
ATL Montagne DOC, Viale Giolitti, 7/9 - 10064 Pinerolo (TO)
Telephone: 0121 794003 - fax 0121 628882
E-mail info@montagnedoc.it

There are more than 100 fortifications in the Olympic Valleys.
The fortress of Fenestrelle, the 'Great Wall of Piedmont',
over 3 km long, is second in length only
to the Great Wall of China

Modern architecture peeps through the pines with a background of sun-kissed mountains.

Bardonecchia's Palazzo delle Feste (once known as the Kursaal) hosts meetings, conferences and shows. The building dominates a great open vista of mountain peaks.

SNOW ITINERARIES

*he fact that the 20ᵗʰ Winter Olympics
are to be hosted by the city of Turin, the surrounding
province and the region of Piedmont in general,
means that we cannot ignore the fact that the white
peaks of the nearby Alps are a haven for lovers
of skiing and, indeed, all winter sports.*

The so-called 'Milky Way' of **Sestriere, Monginevro, San Sicario, Sauze d'Oulx, Claviere and Cesana** offers over 400 km of ski runs and 96 ski lifts linked to one another beneath the sun at 2000 m above sea-level along the Susa and Chisone valleys.

To these towns we must add **Bardonecchia** and **Pragelato**, also Olympic competition sites. The Olympic games, to be held in February 2006, will lead to a complete overhaul of all the ski lifts and connected services, putting Piedmont at the apex of winter sports on a world-wide scale. The Alpine ski races will be held at Sestriere and San Sicario- Fraiteve, Cross country skiing and Ski jumping at Pragelato, and the roofs of Sauze d'Oulx will form a scenic background for the acrobatics of the Free-style ski jumping. San Sicario will host the Biathlon and the Bobsleigh, Luge and Skeleton races will be held at the Pariol hamlet of Cesana. The Snow-board events will be at Bardonecchia.

The indoor winter events (Ice hockey, Figure skating, Speed skating and Short track) will be held in Turin's stadiums. Curling will be at Pinerolo.

The opening and closing ceremonies of the Games with their spectacular choreography and festival of lights will be held in Turin's communal sports centre, renamed 'Olympic Stadium' for the event.

2006 OLYMPIC SYMBOLS

TURIN

Speed skating

Short track - training area

Figure skating - competition - training area

Ice hockey

SUSA VALLEY

SAUZE D'OULX

Freestyle

PRAGELATO

Cross-country skiing

Ski jumping

Northern combined

BARDONECCHIA

Snowboard

(Olympic Village)

SAN SICARIO

Biathlon

Ski racing

Skeleton

Bobsleigh

Luge

SESTRIERE

Ski racing (Skiers residence)

CLAVIERE

Ski racing

Cross-country skiing – training area

CHISONE VALLEY

PINEROLO

Curling

TORRE PELLICE

Training for ice hockey

SPARE TIME

GOLF
TREKKING
CYCLING
SCHOOLS OF CUISINE
WINE TASTING courses
SHOPPING AND RELAXATION
GENERAL INFORMATION

SPARE TIME

*𝒫iedmont offers countless attractions
to complete a holiday dedicated to the pleasures
of the palate. For lovers of the open air, there is
trekking through the woods and vineyards or
cycling over hills and dales. Also on offer is tennis,
golf with greens of international quality, cookery
schools, shopping, evenings out at the discotheque
or a pleasant break in one of Piedmont's
many famous caffes.*

GOLF

lthough this sport has taken root relatively recently in Piedmont, the region already offers a number of top-quality greens.

Every tourist centre offers a green with at least 18 holes and a number of smaller greens where even the most demanding golfer can enjoy his or herself.

GOLF CLUBS:
Golf Club Cherasco (CN) - Loc. Fraschetta
Telephone: 0172 489772 - fax 0172 488489
(18 holes - par 72)

Golf Club La Margherita - 10022 Carmagnola (TO) - Str Pralormo, 29
Telephone + fax 011 9795113 (18 holes - par 72)

Golf Club Santa Croce - Boves (CN) - Fraz. Mellana
Telephone: 0171 387041 - fax 0171 387512 (18 holes - par 72)

Golf Club Villa Carolina - 15060 Capriata d'Orbu (AL) - Via Ovada, 51
Telephone + fax 0143 467355 (27 holes - par 108)

Golf Club i Roveri - 10070 Fiano (TO) - Rotta Cerbiatta, 24
Telephone: 011 9235667 - fax 011 9235669 (27 holes - par 108)

Golf Club Margara - Fubine (AL) - Via Tenuta Margara, 25
Telephone: 0131 778555 - fax 0131 778772 (27 holes - par 108)

Golf Club le Betulle - 13050 Magnano (VC)
Telephone + fax 015 679151 (18 holes par 72)

Golf Club Sestrieres - 10058 Sestrieres (TO) - P.le Agnelli, 4
Telephone + fax 0122 76243
(18 holes - par 67 open from June to September)

Golf Club des Illes Borromees - 28010 Stresa (NO) - Loc Motta Rossa
Telephone + fax 032 3929285 (18 holes - par 72)

Other Golf Clubs are to be found at: Claviere TO, Premeno NO, Valenza AL, and Vinovo TO.

The Claviere Golf Club in the high Susa Valley.

Cross-country skiing at Monginevro:
an unbeatable sense of freedom for the expert and tourist alike.

TREKKING

Every Piedmontese tourist area offers possibilities for the walker at all levels of experience.

Routes through the Langa and Roero regions lead along woodland paths rich in local flora and fauna: this is the land of game, wild mushrooms, truffles and vineyards. Other routes lead through the hazel and fruit groves of the same area.

All the Alpine areas are rich in routes for walkers, often offering the possibility to admire spectacular views from the summit of a mountain, especially those containing morainic lakes, or to follow a stream along its bed through a valley.

FOR FURTHER INFORMATION AND MAPS, CONTACT:
Associazione Trekking in Langa, Ostello del Barbaresco, 2
12051 San Rocco Seno d'Elvio, Alba CN Telephone: 0173 286968

A walk in the woods after a heavy snowfall can be a wonderful experience.

CYCLING

The roads of Piedmont have hosted some of the most spectacular hours of the Giro d'Italia and the Tour de France over the last few decades. Examples are the great champion's solitary arrivals at the summit of Sestriere or mythical breakaways at the Colle dell'Agnello in Cuneo province.

In any case, it is true to say that many areas of Piedmont offer natural cycle runs: from Dogliani to Neive; from Cortemilia to Gavi or from Canale to Cocconato, there is great cycling to be had for enthusiasts.

Whether circular or one-way, these routes are ideal for the lack of traffic and the wonderful views they offer. Some of the routes are variable according to the cyclist's experience.

Easier routes take you along river valleys and more strenuous ones follow the contours of the hills with ascents varying form 4% to 12%.

FOR FURTHER INFORMATION AND MAPS CONTACT:
ACA, Piazza San Paolo, 3 - 12051 Alba CN
Telephone: 0173 226611

SCHOOLS OF CUISINE

It is only natural, given Piedmont's great culinary traditions, that it should offer cookery courses for its tourists.

Many of the numerous professional cookery schools offer courses of 2 or 3 days for the tourist interested in learning the secrets of Piedmontese cuisine accompanied by professional cooks of the region.

Here, you can learn how to prepare a fondue with truffles, the famous ravioli 'del plin', braised beef with Barolo or Grandmother's chocolate pudding, taught by some of the area's most renowned chefs. There's nothing more fun than a cookery course in the company of friends during a pleasant break in Piedmont!

Among the chefs who run courses of Piedmontese cuisine for tourists are:
Carlo Zarri - Hotel Ristorante Villa San Carlo - Cortemilia CN
Elisa Burlotto - Hotel Ristorante Castello di Verduno - Verduno CN
Tonino Verro - Hotel Ristorante La Contea di Neive - Neive CN

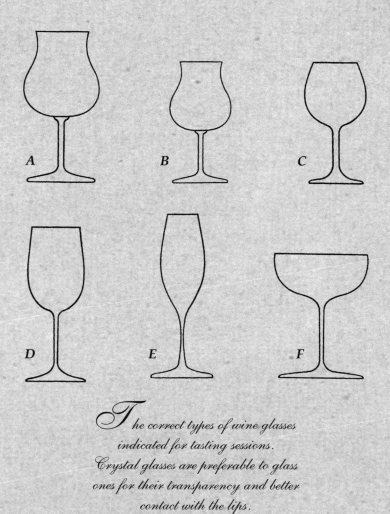

*The correct types of wine glasses
indicated for tasting sessions.
Crystal glasses are preferable to glass
ones for their transparency and better
contact with the lips.*

A large 'Piedmont' glass, for Barolo and Barbaresco.
B small 'Piedmont' glass for Roero and Nebbiolo d'Alba.
C 'tulip' calyx glass for Barbera, Dolcetto, Freisa, Pelaverga, Grignolino and other young red wines.
D light, slim calyx for Favorita, Arneis and other young, dry white wines.
E flute for dry sparkling wines.
F champagne cup for Moscato and Asti Spumante.

WINE TASTING COURSES

Piedmontese wines, as well as its cuisine, merit a closer look maybe at a semi-professional level. There are many courses organised in Piedmont which give wine lovers the opportunity to learn how to taste and appreciate wines such as Barolo, Barbaresco and Barbera.

These are not-to-be-missed opportunities for every lover of excellent wines. Learning how to correctly taste a wine, how to evaluate its characteristics and strong points, how the grapes are grown, methods of production and maturation, is an unforgettable experience.

Some of these courses are held directly by the wine producers themselves. Others are organised by professional sommeliers who are also restaurant or hotel owners.

Courses can be followed at the following:

Carlo Zarri - Hotel Ristorante Villa San Carlo - Cortemilia CN

Mariuccia Borio - Cantina Cascina Castlet - Costigliole AT

FOR FURTHER INFORMATION CONTACT THE TOURIST OFFICE:

Consorzio Turistico Langhe Monferrato e Roero

P.zza Medford, 3 - 12051 Alba (CN) - Telephone: 0173 361538 fax 0173 293600 - e-mail: info@turismodoc.it

HÔTEL CENTRAL & CONTINENTAL

. . . TORINO

G. COLOMBINI, Propr.

WILD & Ci - MILANO 21913

An attractive Art Nouveau menu.

SHOPPING AND RELAXATION

As well as Piedmont's typical alimentary products, there are numerous other opportunities for enjoyable shopping. Articles include gold, furniture, clothing, whether sports attire, elegant or casual wear and articles for the home. Turin's caffès, many of which are of historical or artistic interest, offer moments of peace and quiet.

The best shopping is probably to be found in Piedmont's town centres, both small and large, which are often pedestrian precincts and where articles typical of the area can be acquired during a pleasant stroll. There is also a choice of factory stores where famous brand names can be bought directly. Examples are Zegna or Miroglio, where elegant wear can be found or, if sportswear is desired, Fila or Roba di Kappa. Alessi's factory store sells goods for the home.

Some towns are synonymous with a particular product, such as Valenza and its gold, where everywhere you go you see the shine of bracelets, rings and earrings.

Finally, there are also many shopping centres in Piedmont with brand-name outlets where products can be found at less.

FOR FURTHER INFORMATION:

- Associazione Orafa Valenzana, Piazza Don Minzoni, 1
  15048 Valenza AL - Telephone: 0131 946609
- Fila Italia Outlet Store, Viale Cesare Battisti, 28 - 13900 Biella
  Telephone: 015 23138
- Fratelli Piacenza, Cachemire Outlet Store, Regione Cisi
  13814 Pollone BI - Telephone: 015 6191230
- Outlet di Serravalle, Via della Moda, 1 - 15069 Serravalle Scrivia AL
  Telephone: 0143 609015
- Robe di Kappa Basic Village, Via Foggia, 42 - 10152 Torino TO
  Telephone: 011 26171
- Vestebene Factory Store, Via Santa Margherita, 23 - 12051 Alba
  Telephone: 0173 299111
- Ermenegildo Zegna Outlet Store, Strada Trossi, - 13871
  Sandigliano BI
  Telephone: 015 2496199

Further information on: www.guidaspacci.it

*Part of Turin's 3000 metres of covered walkways.
This photograph is of Via Roma, the main shopping street.*

THE 'ROMAN QUARTER'

This area of Turin's historical centre, between the streets of XX Settembre, Corso Regina Margherita, Via Milano and Garibaldi, has recently been restored to its former glory.

Here, an evening out or a simple stroll to admire the city's historical past can be enjoyed. The area is known as the 'Roman Quarter' because it contains the city's archeological remains, that is, those of the town known as 'Augusta Taurinorum', denoting a young bull, the symbol of which is still to be found on the city's public water fountains. Here, the remains of the great Roman amphitheatre and the Palatine towers, monuments of great rarity, and in excellent state of preservation, can be admired. Here is also, as mentioned before, the cathedral of San Giovanni Battista which conserves the Holy Shroud of Turin.

The 'quadrilatero romano' is interesting also for its restaurants and general 'joie de vivre'. The antique buildings have been carefully restored and the maze of cobbled streets is a fascinating reminder of times past and one of the most attractive parts of the city.

*'I Murazzi', a popular
and fashionable nighttime place
on the banks of the river
Po with its water-lily-style marquis.*

*For lovers of bric-a-brac the 'gran
Balon' is Turin's antiques market,
held every second Sunday of the month at
Borgo Dora. The name derives from
the ballgames once played in the area.
The market dates back to 1735.*

The romantic green heart of Turin, the San Valentino park with its Savoy Castle, on the banks of the river Po.

Piedmont's caffès are an echo of the past when time slipped slowly by. Among the most famous are: Mulassano, San Carlo, Baratti e Milano and Fiorio in Turin; Arione in Cuneo and Calissano in Alba.

GENERAL INFORMATION

- Regional Tourist Agency:
  Agenzia Turistica Regionale
  Via Viotti, 2 - 10121 Torino
  Telephone: 011 55441111 - fax 011 5627176
  e-mail: atrinfo@atr.piemonte.it

- Local Tourist Consortium (Alba):
  Consorzio Turistico Langhe Monferrato e Roero,
  P.zza Medford, 3 - 12051 Alba (CN)
  Telephone: 0173 361538 - fax 0173 293600
  e-mail: info@turismodoc.it

- Turin Airport (Caselle)
  Telephone: 011 5769220
  e-mail: www.turin-airport.com

- Genoa Airport
  Telephone: 010 6015212 - fax 010 6015203
  e-mail: www.marketing@airport.genova.it

- Milan Malpensa Airport:
  Telephone: 02 74852200
  e-mail: www.malpensa-airport.com

- Alitalia,
  Via Lagrange, 35 - 10123 Torino
  Telephone: 011 57691 - fax 011 5769220
  www.alitalia.it

- Italian Trains (Turin Station)
  stazione di Porta Nuova - 10125 Torino
  Telephone: 011 531327 - fax 011 5617095
  www.trenitalia.com

- Italian Automobile Club
  ACI,
  Via Giovanni Giolitti, 15 - 10123 Torino
  Telephone: 011 57791

HOW TO GET TO PIEDMONT

By Air:

Turin Airport (Caselle)

Milan Malpensa airport

Genoa Airport

By Rail:

From Milan towards north Piedmont in the direction of Novara-Turin

From Milan towards south Piedmont in the direction of Milan-Tortona-Alessandria

From Rome: via Florence-Bologna-Turin

From Rome: via Genoa-Alessandria-Asti-Turin

From Nice/Monte Carlo: via Ventimiglia-Savona-Turin

From Paris via Lyon-Turin

From North Europe: via Milan

By Motorway ('Autostrada'):

From Milan towards Turin: the A4

From Milan towards Genoa: the A7 as far as Tortona the A21 for Turin via Alessandria

From Paris: via Lyon through the Frejus tunnel A32

From Rome: A1 to Florence then Bologna – Piacenza then A21 for Turin via Alessandria

From Nice/Monte Carlo: A10 Ventimiglia-Savona then the A26 for Turin

From Basle: the San Gottardo tunnel then the A9 to Milan

From Berne: the Mont Blanc tunnel then the A5 to Aosta

From Munich: the Brennero tunnel then the A22 to Milan

CARLO ZARRI
PIEDMONT: SENSATIONS
'A journey through Piedmont's
garden of delights'.

PREFACE:
Piero Gros

EDITORIAL AND ARTISTIC CONSULTANTS:
Alberto Cottino, Piercarlo Grimaldi,
Giacomo Soncini, Roberto De Gregorio

TRANSLATION:
J. Taylor

PHOTOGRAPHIC REFERENCES:

ATL and the Tourist Offices of: Alessandria, Asti, Biella, Cuneo,
Novara, Langhe and Roero, Verbano Cusio Ossola, Vercelli.

The photographic archives of the Civic Museum of Modern Art
The photographic archives of the Turin Office of Tourism

The Regional agency for Promotion of Tourism in Piedmont

Office du tourisme de Mongenevre (F)

• Studio Reporter TO • Archives of Omega Editions

B. Accomasso - A. Adriano - B. Allaix - D. Alpe - A. Buccolo
E. Canziani - G.P. Cavallero - F. Lava - K. Mejer - B. Necade
A e G. Nicola - P. Gros - C. Zarri.

The museum of the diocese of Susa

The chamber of commerce of Cuneo Astisio (Roero)

ASCOM Alba

The editor is available for any queries regarding copyright for material used in this book.

The author and the editor thank all those who, both directly and indi-
rectly, have contributed to the making of this book. In particular they
would like to thank:
Ricky and Paola, Giovanni Bera, Mauro Carbone, Ferruccio
Dardanello, Elisabetta Grasso, Paola Musolino, Fabrizio Pace, Katia
Robaldo, Daniela Silvestrin, Mirko Usseglio, Claudio Vaccaneo,
Daniela Viberti, Mariuccia Viglino, Patrizia Bonifacio, Silvana Rabino

INDEX

SUGGESTIONS ON HOW TO USE THIS BOOK

There are many ways of interpreting a book.

To render the perusal of this book even more pleasurable, we decided to let the images 'speak' for the text, aiming almost for a 'hypertext' which can be read taking various different 'routes':

First route: the simplest and most immediate, obtained by following the images presented in the book with their captions. Among these, may be found paintings, especially by Piedmontese artists, antique prints, historical or contemporary photographs.

Second route: the text is divided into 2 parts using the same characters. The first and most evident part is a resume of the contents of the chapter.

Third route: this is the longest of the three, allowing the reader to read and appreciate the volume's meaning in its entirety, through its text and images. The title of each chapter is printed on the top of each page for easy reference.

Happy reading!

THE AUTHOR

Carlo Zarri was born in Albenga in 1965. After obtaining a diploma in Tourism Studies at the Technical Institute 'G. Leopardi' of Bergamo, at the age of 20, he and his family moved to Cortemilia where he could develop his passion for fine food and wine and enjoy with others all the fine things that Piedmont has to offer. He travels the world taking part in conferences, gaining experience in the area of tourism and collecting new ideas for his profession.

Carlo is a professional sommelier. His greatest pleasure is astonishing the clients of his family's hotel-restaurant with his culinary prowess. For the past few years, he has been president of the Consortium of Tourism for Langhe, Monferrato and Roero. He is also a consultant for the 2006 Olympics Committee in Turin.

LIONS CLUB

Our most heart-felt thanks to the
1081A3 group of the Lions Club International
and especially the Lions Club 'Cortemilia e Valli',
who are donating the Royalties from this book to charity.
Thanks also to Monsignor Giuseppe Pellerino,
missionary with the Combonian Fathers in Sudan,
for the building of the schools and aqueducts
indispensable for the survival of this country's people.

End of printing
October 2004
Typeset by Camedda & C. s.n.c Turin